FREEDOM
THE IRENE HOANG STORY
an autobiography

FREEDOM

THE IRENE HOANG STORY

An Autobiography

Author Irene Hoang

Published by Melbourne Education & Training Centre Pty Ltd
U904 95 Charlotte Street, Brisbane QLD 4000 Australia

ISBN: 978-1547001644

Kindle and paperback available on Amazon.com Kindle store

Vietnamese edition available on Amazon.com and Createspace.com

Additional bulk copies available by contacting:

Irene Hoang on irenehoangmlm@gmail.com

Or via the publisher

Melbourne Education & Training Centre Pty Ltd
www.melbourneeducationandtrainingcentre.com
WhatsApp +61404178126
Email info@melbourneeducationandtrainingcentre.com

TABLE OF CONTENTS

Foreword

It has been my great pleasure to see Irene succeed in life. Her dedication to achieving her results has led to massive action on a scale never seen before.

She has broken business building records. She has worked harder than anyone I have ever met. She has turned around failures time and time again and come back even stronger.

I know the future for Irene is bright. She takes advice from those whom she respects, and I have been lucky enough to be in the position to share some of my success secrets with her.

I have also been able to identify past patterns she has changed to create a 180-degree transformation in her professional results.

I am proud to see her continuing to learn and grow and create great teams internationally.

This book is a road map for success for anyone wanting a way out of their problems. It is an inspiration to women everywhere. And it proves anything is possible.

It is a clear path to being responsible and taking control of your destiny, and it is full of the direction for you to have a life of your own freedom in all aspects of life.

Anonymous

What people are saying

Irene is a leader who makes her success look easy. But you know she has worked hard for it. I am amazed to read about her challenges from such a young age and how she continues to bounce back. She deserves everything she has created. Anyone wanting a role model for never giving up needs to read this book.

Tom "Big Al" Schreiter
Author of the Big Al books and Network Marketing Legend.
www.BigAlBooks.com

This is an amazing leadership book about how a woman was able to achieve her freedom through transforming her personal struggle and applying herself through skill.

Irene's life story is an example to women across the world. She inspires with her personal story starting as a young gymnast and then connects the dots all the way to her successes into business world.

The lessons in this book for anyone in business, but especially women are timeless and inspiring. A must read for every entrepreneur!

Masa Cemazar
Entrepreneur and Founder
Pyjamabosses.com

My friend Irene is such a legend. I knew the minute she would write a book it would have golden nuggets of wisdom in it. I could not know how much more I know now since reading it. Her life has been an amazing set of challenges that only she could overcome.

I am glad to have her as a friend and over the years I have watched her matured to be a formidable leader capable of leading a huge group beyond her own country of Vietnam.

I wish every young entrepreneur would read this book and save them so much pain and agony! They can see the secret right away in this book.

Raymond Tay
Professional Network Marketer
www.raymondtay.com

Introduction

This is a book about freedom.

The freedom I found after twenty-four years in traditional business, working hard, and almost dying.

A lot of people in Vietnam think I'd died already, because they thought what I'd gone through was so much and so bad.

But after moving from Hanoi to Ho Chi Minh City, I came back from the dead and started again..

I wrote this book to tell my story so younger people choosing jobs can have more choices.

This book about my business life will help businessmen and businesswomen who need the motivation to not give up.

Most of all, it is for people who want to be financially free, for people who want time freedom and have the health to enjoy it.

It is about being hungry for money, using it well, and working to achieve your goals and dreams.

It is a book about changing our focus to what is important.

It is about the mistakes I have made in my life, and the things I have learned along the way.

It is about finding a mentor to listen to, someone you respect, then taking their advice and acting on it.

This book is about sharing how I'd reached the point of having the freedom to choose how I live my life, and showing you how you can do it, too.

This book is my personal journey about working hard and generating active income.

It is a book about the power of passive income and how, once you understand it, you will do anything to get it.

It is a book about surrounding yourself with the people you need to get you to where you need to be—mentors, coaches, leaders.

It is a book about values and ethics, and the power of your family to motivate and inspire you.

It is a book about your attitude. It will help you to laser focus to be sure you are looking for the right thing, and then to take the right steps toward it.

When we combine it all together, we will have a guide for transforming your life.

Why do I want to share my life and lessons with you?

Because I have achieved freedom.

Freedom means having success in life in these three areas at the same time:

Time freedom
Financial Freedom
Health Freedom

But it was not always that way. I will show you what I did wrong and what I did right. After twenty-four years of living what I thought was my life's purpose and passion, I ended up in the hospital and lost everything.

This life-defining crisis changed everything for me.

As I lay in a bed in Boston, halfway around the world from my family and friends, I wondered: Will I ever see them again?

I cannot explain how devastated I was at that moment. I

had the time to look back on my life and realize I had none of the three components of a happy life.

I had a business that was falling apart, and no cash flow.

I was working twenty-four-seven and not seeing my family or friends.

I had a life-threatening condition in a hospital.

What changed for me?

What made the difference for me in just five short years to become a millionaire flying first class around the world with my family?

What made the difference for me to fit more into my schedule, to achieve more, and to see the people who are important to me?

What made the difference for me to have the healthy life I needed to live it one hundred percent?

What made the difference?

I changed my focus.

Instead of focusing on what to do, I focused on where I wanted to be.

Instead of focusing on making money, I focused on how much money I needed, then took the necessary action.

Instead of managing my time, one day at a time, I looked at how I wanted to spend my time and changed how I spent each day.

Instead of working to make money so I could spend time with my family, I set a goal for spending time with my family, and I made everything else work around them.

Instead of fitting food and nutrition around my life, they became a part of every meal.

Instead of hoping my body would survive a busy schedule, I chose to be healthy and then listened to my body. Now, I feed it what it needs.

And I learned to listen to a mentor who wanted me to have a happy life.

A mentor who had everything I wanted in life.

I took the time to listen, to change my focus, and to act in a whole new way.

Now I have the freedom to fly anywhere in the world, at anytime, first class.

I have the freedom to drive around in my yellow Lamborghini or in my black Rolls Royce.

I have the freedom to stay in any five-star hotel in the world, for as long as I want.

I have the freedom to order in a Michelin-star restaurant and not worry about the price.

I have the freedom to support children—my own and others.

I have the freedom to spend time with my children.

I have the freedom to mentor and to teach my organization the principles I have mastered.

I have the freedom to do this, because my health is at 100%.

What is the key to this freedom?

Unlocking a principle based on years of research and common sense, and finally applying it to my life.

The key was stopping the bad work and money habits I'd carried around in business for twenty-four years. I am serious; they nearly killed me. Focusing on the result and creating the necessary actions have helped me to create new habits of action.

The key was creating optimum health solutions for me and my family. I want to live a long time so we can enjoy the success that financial freedom has created. Focusing on giving my body what it needs helps me to feel great all the time.

The key was managing my time under my own schedule and spending it with who I want, where I want, for as long as I want. Focusing on what is important and not compromising—ever.

Let me share my story with you…

Young Life

Growing up and Gymnastics

When I was young, I loved to do gymnastics.

Sport and exercise was something I'd loved to do ever since I could walk. Cartwheels and somersaults, everywhere I went.

I would sing and dance and spin and turn. I loved to watch dancers and gymnasts on the TV, and I copied their every move.

At kindergarten, every time we had a break, I was out on the grass doing handstands, falling over, practicing and getting my balance.

One day, someone spotted me having fun in the park. They approached my parents and talked to them about sending me to a school where my talent could be developed. Imagine the joy on my mother's and family's faces when they could share with their friends how proud they were. Their daughter had been invited to such a prestigious opportunity. One day, maybe she would represent Vietnam at the Olympics or the World Championships. This would bring great honour to the family.

My parents were happy for me to be fit, strong, and healthy. So after a quick discussion, focusing on the positives of the future, they agreed to send me to the school.

I was accepted in to learn gymnastics. In some countries, it would be seen as the equivalent of an institute of sport, where people are hand-selected to be trained as professional athletes. In Vietnam, it was a full-immersion experience, where we not only did our schooling, but also trained to represent our country in different sports in a rigorous and disciplined environment.

A part of why my parents were able to send me was because they were rich. Without this, we could not have afforded the training program, the accommodation, and the specialized coaching.

Our country was a poor country at this time, coming out at the end of a very long war. This was a time to focus on showing the world we had culture, purpose, and a competitive spirit.

But our country did not have very much money to pay for these schools and institutes, so only the wealthy sent their children, and they subsidized the development of the future athletes of my country.

Independence

My parents already knew that I, at just six years old, would be able to be independent and thrive on the opportunity in front of me.

This involved moving from my home, to the school in the city—to be a boarder living in a strange place, and to live with a group of girls all training to be the next Olympic medalist in their chosen sports.

Now, I have to tell you, if you do not know, gymnastics is very tough sport. Tough on the body, and tough to be the best. There is a lot of competition, and there are a lot of reasons you do not become competitive or successful.

I am not sure what your schooling was like when you were six years old, but this is how my day went:

The program was quite rigid, and the routine was something I remember to this day.

Get up every morning at five a.m. Summer, winter, autumn, and spring.

We would do outdoor exercise, no matter what the time of the year.

Often, there was snow on the ground as we did our running, jumping, and strength-building exercises. Military boot camps are for adults; we were just children.

The weak would drop very quickly. They would complain, they would get ill, and they would be sent home. And never be seen again.

I knew early on that I had to be strong to survive here. And to succeed, I would need to use all of the skills I had in mental toughness, resilience, and self-belief.

I would not have my parents there each night, giving me the reassurance and support. It would have been impossible without being strong.

I had to grow up very quickly.

I had to develop the ability to solve problems, manage my emotions, and handle being homesick and missing my parents.

Showing weakness in these areas only meant they trained you harder.

At 7:30 a.m., we would go to school like other children in Hanoi. The focus on sport, training, and learning was always the top priority. But the regular school subjects like language and maths and science were seen as equally important to create a balanced schooling. Everyone knows that after a sports career is over, you will need other skills and specialized areas to fall back on. So they did look after us in this way.

Two p.m. was time for training again. This time, we were indoors, in the gymnasium. We learned to stretch, to develop our flexibility, and to become familiar with the apparatus. At my age, I had never seen the equipment before. I did not know how any of it worked. I had never seen them or used them, so it was all new.

Somehow, they saw talent in me and believed I could work to become successful.

I learned to use the balance beam, the vault, the uneven

bars, and to do the floor routines. I was so small, some of them I could not even reach.

But I learned their dimensions, their key elements, and practiced and practiced.

This was the first time in my life people had seen my potential and had assisted me and encouraged me.

In the outside world, ever since those early days, I have had to prove people wrong when they say "You can't do it," even inside the school as a teenager and especially when it came to competitions.

In the business world, it has been the same. But more about that later.

Training meant having a coach. Coaching in the sport of gymnastics is about assisting a young girl to see her potential, then pushing her almost to the breaking point. The breaking point in their body, that is, and the breaking point in their mind about what is possible for their body to do.

I thrived on the coaching. I loved that someone who knew my ability could take me, mould me, and make me better if I followed their instructions.

Being coached was also a big part of my learning to be independent. When I realized the coach did not do the exercise, that it was just me, I knew I, rather than the coach, would get the medals. This was to be my moment. I would shine in the competitions and get the medals around my neck. I would show my parents, my family, and friends I could achieve amazing things.

But something nagged in the back of my mind for a few years. I did not know why my parents had sent me to this camp. They did not need me to learn fitness, just for the sake of it; I could do that at home and at a regular school.

I found out from my classmates and from the competition that most young girls were sent there because they wanted to be professional sportspersons and to earn their own money to send back to their families, winning sponsorships and competitions in order to send the money home. But my parents did not need the money an athlete could make. This was the way it was in Vietnam. Children or young people who became successful in anything would send their winnings back to the parents who had sacrificed for them to go train.

But again, my parents did not need that. While I trained and trained away from my family, I would wonder why, week after week.

When I turned ten years old, I realized why I was sent away to gymnastics school.

I understood with a sense of calm and peace what had been bothering me for so long, because now I could look back and see what I had achieved, and how I had done it.

My parents wanted me to be strong and independent.

The challenges I would face living away from home would make me stronger, not weaker.

The discipline and routine of sport training would be good for me in my future personal and professional life.

Something in my personality had shown them, even when I was a very young girl. They knew this path would be okay for me, that the experience would help me to grow and shine.

And now I looked ahead with hope for the future to be the best in the entire school. I was always striving. In my spare time, I was training, always learning to be better. I had the work ethic to be the best. Not everyone liked this, of course; they wanted to start talking about boys, and fashion, and their future away from the school.

And even my friends started to be jealous of me. They attacked me. They said terrible things.

"You cannot be successful."

"You can't win."

"You can't be number one."

"You can't be a professional."

13

It is hard when the people around you stop believing in you, and even sabotage your dreams. They try to steal them away from you.

By then, I knew this would happen. And I'd expected it, after so much competition and practice and time together.

But I had my own philosophy.

"If you think you never can win, you would quit early. If you think one day you can win, you set a goal, and you go for the goal."

No matter what.

This mindset helped me to get through people saying I could not do it.

The attitude I had helped me if I performed well but did not win a competition, or if I did not feel like training and performing.

I had a philosophy back then, and I still do now.

I always listen to what people say. If someone says I can't do something, I say I can.

I always did the opposite of what people said about me, and what I could and could not do.

If I heard someone say "Irene, you can't be a winner," I reversed their statement to: "Irene, you are a winner!"

It is about controlling your mindset.

When I knew people would try to bring me down, I made winning my obsession. My only goal. This did not win me friends; it made me more enemies. But I continued to win, and to be the best.

I learned I was #1 at our school, but my coach at the time did not like me. So they put me in the standard team and made me go as the second best group of gymnasts. This challenged me to not just do well, but to beat everyone; it reflected on them more than it did on me if I did better than anyone else.

Mostly, I just wanted to do my best, and the results would show.

I trained harder. I applied myself to the singular focus on my goal of being the best in the school, the city, the country.

When I attended my first national tournament, I had just one goal in my mind.

WIN!

I wanted it, I knew I could win.

I had a strong expectation of only one possible outcome, winning.

I had total self-confidence in my ability to win.

And a strong self-belief based on my disciplined practice and rehearsal of winning.

I had trained for a long time to win.

I was the best at my school, I would always win.

I was intimidating. Everyone around me was in awe of my discipline, my training, my exercise habits. They quietly admired my refusal to let outside circumstances distract me from my goal.

And at the national tournament—I won all four categories.

I surprised everyone—but me.

For four years I had been training on the vault, the uneven bars, the balance beam, and the floor.

I had fallen over so many times. I had many injuries. But I got up. And I healed.

Every morning at five a.m., I was up and exercising. Rain, snow, sun, and wind—it didn't matter.

Every morning, between fitness and skill training sessions, we had academic studies. Feeding my mind as well as my body was important, so we had a balanced education.

And when we went back to exercise and training in the afternoon, I trained longer than everyone else. I worked harder than everyone else. I wanted to be better than everyone else.

I was fit, skillful, strong, and determined.

If I was going to compete, there was only one goal I could see.

Win

Winning was the goal and the result I worked toward as soon as I saw a goal to achieve. Having an end goal helps to teach you what you need to do in order to achieve it.

Of course, at the age of six or seven, you do not know what winning means. A ribbon, a medal, some praise from the adults around you is nice. Getting your parents' approval is nice. Maybe you get a nod from a coach who would see the results of your hard work.

But the biggest decision I realized early in my time at the school was if I choose to win, I can win.

From a very young age, I've had the dream to be a professional athlete. I wanted to be a professional, and have what they have. Back then I could see that, in the future, I could represent my country around the world. Being the best in the world.

One day, I could go to the Olympics and win a gold medal there, too.

So, after that first national championship, I continued to train even more. I continued to get better. I continued to get stronger.

And I continued to win. I became very famous. I was the national champion of Vietnam. This was a high achievement, and sports people were looked up to around the country.

I was a celebrity in this sport and was taken to many towns and cities to show how good our school was at creating champions.

Everyone in my family was proud of me. I had dedicated their life to showing the world how successful Vietnamese athletes could be. And I was one of those athletes. It was getting exciting and the future looked amazing.

Gymnastics gave our country a chance to be on the world stage and to show how good we were.

Because you have to realize, after many years of war and division, Vietnam needed a reason to celebrate. We worked so hard to show we were united, positive, and wanting to change how we were seen.

So for me, I felt like I was a part of a new generation of looking to the good things and showing what we could achieve. Showing that we could be focused on personal achievements. For me, this meant representing my country.

Personal effort.
Discipline.
Hard work.
Focus.
Goals.

Soon the chance to bring it all together would arrive.

China

When I was fifteen, I was preparing for an international gymnastics tournament scheduled in China.

I was training harder than I ever had.

I wanted to prove to my parents, my coach, my school how worthwhile the investment in me over all this time was.

This was my chance to be on the international stage. To show everyone how the best of the best in Vietnam could achieve success in gymnastics. To show a new face for our country that had suffered so much in our reputation around the world.

Every morning, I would wake up with the goal of winning GOLD in China.

I woke up after dreams of standing on the podium. I could hear the national anthem of Vietnam ringing through the stadium.

I saw my mother smiling and applauding me from the crowd.

And I could see my coach nodding in approval.

So I trained longer hours.

Anytime one of my teammates said I wasn't going to win, I worked harder.

Anytime my coach said I was not working hard enough, I worked harder.

I took every negative and focused on training harder.

I took every doubter and their bad attitude and increased my own self-confidence.

I did not think of anything other than winning in China.

One morning, I started training, but I wasn't feeling quite 100%.

I was warming up, feeling unfocused and distracted.

Maybe my hormones were messing with my mind; as a fifteen-year-old girl, you have a lot going on, and I was no different.

Despite my incredible focus on my sport, my body was changing.

I was making the transition from girl to woman, and with

boys starting to catch my eye, I felt things I had never felt before. Today was not the day to think about boys, and I pushed the thoughts out of my mind.

This morning, my mind was definitely wandering, which was unusual for me.

After my warm up, I went out and practiced on the uneven bars, and everything was going well.

But I didn't stick any of my landings the way I normally would. It was frustrating me. Routines I had performed so many times before were now not working.

I did some vault, and I loved the thrill of sprinting at full speed. I widened my eyes, launched onto the trampoline, then jumped, twisted, somersaulted, and flew through the air. I cannot describe it, unless you can imagine everything going into slow motion until my landing. Then the rush of adrenaline and breath returns. You give a big smile, and a thank you to the judges and the crowd with a bow in their direction.

Today as I practiced, I was not landing well. I was overshooting my landing, or finishing short and thudding onto the mat as my legs and then my bottom hit the mat.

Time after time I tried, but I just couldn't get it right the way I would on any other day.

Finally, I went to the beam.

The balance beam is five meters long, 125 centimeters off the ground, and only ten centimeters wide. You have to learn it very young.

When you learn the beam, you have very small feet. You are trained to land on the balls of your feet and toes, pivoting and balancing and jumping and somersaulting.

As you grow, your muscle memory can put your feet where they need to be for the routine. Jumping to do the splits, somersaults, and twists. It takes a lot of practice and a lot of bruises.

Of course, the impact of landing on the beam, solid wood, as you spin and jump, puts incredible pressure on your joints, from your toes, to your ankles, up to the knees and the hips.

This is why we start it so young, to build the strength in the muscles and the tendons. To build the legs into the shape they need to be to handle this unnatural action. But it is unforgiving on the weak and ends the career of many aspiring gymnasts.

This was what I had to work on the most. And I loved the challenge. Knowing how hard it was, I made a point of being the best in our school.

While other people never mastered the beam, I thrived on it. When I won the national championships, my score outshone the second and third place winners.

This is a part of my personality. I had always loved, and I still do, taking the hardest challenge and mastering it. There is no competition at the hardest end of any discipline. Most people give up much earlier.

So, after not feeling well all morning in training, the beam was to be my re-connection to my goal of winning in China. To recommit myself to the focus, determination, and achievement I was known for.

So I began my routine.

Everything went well, and I landed perfectly, to finish with a bow.

Because it went so well, I thought I would do it again. When you do something well, you build your confidence. When you repeat it, then you reinforce that feeling of success. Repeated well enough times, it becomes almost automatic to do it right.

So I had a great second routine. I was doing so well and feeling so good about my domination as the best at this apparatus for so many years, I decided to do one more round.

After the slow start earlier in training, I was now in the zone. I was on fire, untouchable, and the energy around me sparkled like electricity.

People watched me as the senior member of the squad. They copied me, aspired to be like me. Every day after training, the young kids would ask me questions. Every spare moment, they wanted me to watch them practice and give them tips.

My heart was beating faster than ever. After two aggressive rounds on the beam, I was breathing hard. I was sweating and needed more chalk for my hands and feet.

The bandages strapping my feet were holding firm, but the blood showed through my veins of my swollen feet.

I clapped my hands together.

And with a big crowd of my peers, coaches, and the next generation of students watching, I began the routine again.

It was going great. My jumping splits were perfect; I felt like I was floating in mid-air.

I twisted, I somersaulted, I did the finesse work, and I did the strength poses.

Finally, the dismount. I wanted everyone to applaud and admire their best athlete, the one who would bring home the gold in China.

I prepared, leaned back, breathed in deeply, and started my run.

Back flip, back flip, jump, and double somersault dismount, straining and stretching with every bit of energy I had left.

As I came through the second somersault, I intuitively felt I was close to the beam. Too close.

In one sickening crack, my foot caught the edge of the beam. The sound echoed throughout the training gymnasium.

One more crack, and I landed in a mess of arms and legs, and rolled onto my side.

My cry rose up through my throat as I reached for my foot, in shock that I had not landed properly.

But my arm hurt, too, with a sharp, stabbing pain.

Then I realized, with the pain starting to grow, the throbbing and the agony getting more and more intense, that my foot was broken and so was my arm.

After all my practice and training and perfection in execution of every move, I was now broken.

A break is not the end of the world if it is on the shin, because the bone heals and becomes stronger. But it was not high on my shin, it was below the ankle, right in the middle of my foot. Where all the small bones are. Where you cannot set the bone.

I knew immediately that this was the end. No one recovers from a broken foot to compete again. And no one can exercise the rest of their body with a broken arm.

This was a career-ending injury.
I went into shock.

My body hurt more than it had ever hurt before. I could hardly see, my tears were coming so fast. My foot, my arm, the throbbing, and all of the people suffocating me with their tears and cries and organizing a trip to the hospital. I wanted to disappear.

I forget what happened next. Maybe I fainted or passed out. The next few hours were a blur that no one has replayed for me. It is probably so painful, I shut out any memory.

Only in the following days did I get the confirmation of how bad it was. The X-rays proved to the specialists I would never do gymnastics competitively again. It would take enough time to walk. Maybe running would not happen, either.

So a new kind of shock set in. The pain was gone, but the shock of losing my dreams hit me like a locomotive.

Hour by hour, the realization grew that I was no longer the best gymnast on the team. I wasn't even the worst.

I was no longer on the team.

Nine years of schooling and training and coaching was good for nothing in my future.

I had never competed overseas, and now I never would.

This new kind of shock and anger was now directed at myself because my last routine had been anything but perfect and I should have stopped after the second routine.

And a new life would have to begin.

I never went to the international championships.

And I never went to the Olympics.

My dreams were destroyed in one split-second. One mistake. One fall.

I would have to create a new dream, a new goal, and a new life.

So what did I do next?

Business Life

The world of business

Business affected my life from the earliest days.

My mentor asked me to think back to the earliest days and see how I created my beliefs about money. I have always been happy to talk about money because it has always been in my life. And when it was not, I still talked about it, because I wanted it to come back.

I know one thing for sure, and this will be a theme throughout my book, since it is what helps make my life work for me and my extended family.

Having money is better than having no money.
Rich is better than poor.

My parents money ran out and gave me my first taste of life not being fair, and moving from a life where I had everything I wanted, to a life where nothing was easy anymore.

From what I remember, my father had been a successful merchant and trader. Dealing in rice, commodities, and all manner of trade items.He was a professional trader.
He was a merchant. Sold rice, clothing—anything.
He bought and sold commodities, and enjoyed trading.
He was very active in the community and would find what people needed.

When I was young, I remember feeling my family was very rich. Everything we did as a family was luxurious. We

24

ate in good restaurants. Our home was lovely. We had enough of everything. I never had to worry about clothes, because I wore the latest fashion. I never had to worry about anything.

I was very happy with my family. I felt loved and cared for. We lived in Hanoi, in Vietnam. And at the end of the 1960's, the war had been getting more destructive, with large parts of my city destroyed. Then I was born in January of 1970. I did not know I would be growing up at the end of a war that had begun in 1955. It was not until I was five years old that most of the country was stable again. Meanwhile, millions of people were dead. Tens of thousands had left my country as immigrants for other parts of the world.

I also had no idea the impact the war would have on my family and my parents' relationship. Their businesses would suffer. It was a very tough time.

Vietnam was finishing a very long war, and the fighting happened right on our doorstep. It was a terrible time. I was too young to remember most of it, but war affected the entire country. The war surrounded us—on TV, in the streets—and with every passing day, things got worse. The eventual fall of Saigon and the rebuilding process that began in the years that followed was hard. It had a ripple effect through every family and every business.

Across the country, many things changed.

I remember the day my father came in and said he was bankrupt. The international markets had dried up; the customers he used to have couldn't afford his products, and he couldn't afford to buy more things.

This affected my lifestyle, my freedom, and my choices.

Without the financial freedom, I could not choose the university I wanted, and because of the financial failures, I had fewer choices to take my own life to the next level through work and study. The options I wanted were gone.

This was my first lesson in failure and how the lack of money can affect what you want to do.

The control I thought I had over my future was a mirage; I had none at that moment.

It was also my first big shock about life not turning out the way you wanted.

Sometimes plans change due to things beyond your control.

How could I know my parents' money would run out?

How could I know their relationship would suffer to the point of divorce?

How could I know my mother would have me return from my gymnastics school with a career-ending injury?

Life happens in strange ways to take us to the next step in our journey.

Life after the bankruptcy and divorce changed quickly:

No longer were we eating at the restaurants we used to go to every night; we were now cooking at home.

No longer traveling; we worked every day of the week.

Not even driving the car because of the cost of fuel, and then not having a car at all; and Hardest of all, not shopping at our favourite stores to save every possible cent.

I was experiencing shock in so many areas of my life. It was such a dramatic thing for me to see the dreams and goals of my mother and myself snatched away.

Life turned upside down, from having plenty of everything, to near-poverty in just a few months.

Until then, we based all of our goals on having the money to do what we wanted.

And in those days, money had been available.

There was no thought of it ever running out.

So we did not think about struggle.
We did not think about running out of things.

For the first time in my life, I was desperate for my old life, but there was not enough money to buy what I used to have. I could see what I wanted. I could remember the good life. I saw other people having it, and I got angry at the world for turning out so badly for me.

There had to be something I could do to change it, but in the final years of high school, I was pretty self-obsessed. You can imagine a girl who had been at the top of the national gymnastics team now a bitter teenager recuperating from a career-ending injury and hating the world. I had emotions, and I shared them out loud with anyone I could. I caused a few problems for other people, and my mother had to come to the school a few times.

The next phase of our life became something I could not have imagined, even in a nightmare.

I had a lot of questions, and everyone was to blame.

Why did it happen?
Why did it happen to me?
Why couldn't I have everything I wanted in life?
Whose fault is it?

Why did I feel this way?

Because I wanted someone else to take care of me.
Because I thought money would always be there.
Because I wanted everything the way it had been before.
Looking back is always "the good old days."
Before the injury.
Before my parents broke up.
Before we were poor.

Here is one undeniable principle of being poor:

From the moment the money ran out, life became simpler, because it had to. There was no way we could complicate it by buying a lot of things, because we couldn't afford it.

And there was no way we could travel anymore, because another issue had come up.

Sickness

My mother started to get sick, which affected the decisions I was about to make now that school was over.

My mother always had a compassionate Buddhist approach to life. She was a caring and grounded person with a philosophy to help people. She taught me to help people, especially when they could not help themselves.

When someone has no money and they cannot pay you back, then you have to be responsible for them, so we had always been generous in our business and personal life.

My mother realized that life was up and down and up and down, so nothing got her too excited, and nothing got her depressed.

I remember when I was young, she did a lot of charitable donations. She put her philosophy into action, and her focus on social justice involved not just helping out with money, but also helping out with her time.

She was always very professional and looked good. She was the wife of a successful merchant for many years and knew impressions made a difference in business.

When she was alive, I didn't think about her as much, but when she died, I realized how much I had learned from her. I looked at the way I helped people, only to realize—I had become her.

She was my greatest mentor and teacher. I learned everything from her, and those things I use even today help me to be even more successful.

I have become my mother, in all the good ways; I know

she was strong. I wish I could be as good as her, and I hope I can be good to her memory and hold to her standards.

Making the hard decisions

When I went in a new direction, it was because my mum had said it was time to let go of gymnastics.

It was impossible to get back to the top, so it didn't make sense my trying to train just to be disappointed.

She told me to go to university and do something new. Start a new chapter in my life. Create a new dream, a new journey, a new destination.

When I agreed to study at university, though, there was just one problem.

No money. And my mother was sick. I couldn't afford to go, and I couldn't afford to leave her.

So we had a big talk about the future.

Option one

Go to university.

If I did this, it would take all of my mum's money and she'd have nothing left—no security, no safety net, nothing to help if she had problems. And she was alone, too, so it would have been a big choice to leave her and go live my life. She was sick, with no one to look after her.

If I left and something happened, I could have never forgiven myself.

Doing it would be such a big thing that would make me regret it for the rest of my life, even though she was pushing me to do it, which made it even harder.

What made it even more complicated was she was pushing me to go, to leave the country.

She did not want to me to go to a Vietnamese university. She worried about the lifestyle of the students. She worried that I would not be able to focus on my studies. She knew boys and girls spent time together there, so many people influencing naive young girls like me.

She knew I'd become a flighty, soft, romantic girl.

Yes, I am naive. I'll admit I was then, and I am even now. When you are not strong, it is easy to fall in love and do anything a man says. And I was so naive. All of my strength was in my competition, my gymnastics, my health, and my fitness.

But in this situation, I had no choice. I knew it, even if she was sacrificing herself for me. But there was no way I could leave her alone. If I was to go to university, I would go to one locally and work part-time to bring in money.

Even though my mother was sick, she was strong. She gave me an ultimatum: If I went to a local university, I could not have her money. I would have no money and be studying as a pauper. Or I could go to another university in Ho Chi Minh City, or Singapore, or Bangkok.

She wanted to give her life to me so I could have have the university degree she dreamt I wanted and could change my life.

Inside my head I was torn. How could I cause my mother pain, and maybe even lose her? How could I leave her sick and poor?

I consider another option, one that meant I would be the one making a short-term sacrifice to care for my mother and take care of things.

Option two

Get a job.

The idea of work was not a problem for me. I had lived and taken care of myself since I was a small child—more than ten years away from home, managing myself, looking after my diet, my fitness regime, my schooling. It was all a responsibility I had taken for myself. Work would be the same. Follow the plan, be on time, do a good job.

And all the way up until now, I had been continuing to learn. Any lack of success is because I have not learned enough. I am always hungry to learn.

Having a job could mean money to help my mother. Going to university was selfish and it would take me away from my mother.

We both knew going to university would give me amazing opportunities, accelerate my choices, and help me to separate myself from everyone else.

But deep down I knew … "I just cannot leave my mother."

There was no thought of leaving.

I chose to get a job.

My sacrifice for a higher purpose.

This decision would shape my future in ways I could not imagine. I had no idea it would make me one of the most recognized faces in Vietnam.

I chose the beauty industry. The personal care of the Hanoi women. I would do nails. I would take the passion I had for the world of gymnastics and focus it in a new direction, giving manicures and pedicures, and doing the best job possible to make my mother proud and bring in money for us.

I didn't realize it at the time, but I was lucky to get a boss who was tough, a perfectionist.

This meant I had to focus on everything she taught me. To learn quickly. I had to learn to do it right, and then to learn to do it perfectly.

I learned to work hard and resigned myself to the fact I would make this my vocation and my career.

From the age of seventeen, my routine in the nail salon was as demanding as it was in gymnastics.

It was a sense of deja vu in a different career, light years away from the sports world.

Now, I had a new schedule, starting at five a.m., waking up to begin my day. It was not easy. It was not fun. But I had the mindset to make it work because I had to care for my mother and myself, and this was the path I had chosen.

By 5:30, I was at the salon, helping to set up for the day, and I worked and worked. Sometimes I stayed until 11 p.m. or 12 midnight.

It was just as hard as the days I had spent exercising my body and my mind for routines. Now, I was repeating a new routine, with new patients and clients every hour, from the rich and famous to the even more rich and famous.

I was learning a business model—a way to spend my time to exchange it for money.

All I saw all day were feet. I was seventeen years old and very small. Some of the people I did pedicures for were bigger, stronger. Some had the heaviest legs, and they put them on me while I did the work. But I kept my mouth closed. And worked. I put up with it all.

I got very tired working the long days.
But I also got very strong.
I was proving to myself I could get through anything. That nothing would stop me. I would meet my goal. I would take care of my mother.

And this became a theme throughout my life, from gymnastics, to the beauty industry, to what I do today:

Don't tell me I can't do it. I will prove to you I can.

With this salon, we attracted clients who had money. They were coming to the first salon in Hanoi to take advantage of this new manicure and pedicure service. They wanted to show off to their friends in their social circles.

They were all high-level, 'kept' women who never worked, they used their time to spend their husbands' money.

These women were cruel to me. If I did something wrong, or the brushing of the nail polish was not perfect, they hit me!

Their violence taught me about the vanity and ego of my clients. It taught me to do a good job, and it taught me that people would pay a high price for a high quality service. I knew the key to this job was perfection—if I was detailed, took my time, and was patient, I would produce a great job. Then they would tip me well and tell their friends to request me when they visit.

My boss was also very good at the fine details, so she knew I could provide the same standard of service. I rose very quickly through the salon to become the leading beauty therapist.

My boss had come from the rural areas and was making a name for herself with this new nail salon.

She knew you would only get one chance with the clients, which was why she was so tough on us to do a great job.

She also realized that the best marketing for the salon was for everyone in the salon to look good. Our nails had to look amazing. Our makeup immaculate. Our hair perfect.

Nails we could do for each other, and our makeup was a personal process. But our hair needed professional work. And it was a challenge.

Within a few months, I realized another market untapped

33

for our salon: Hairdressing. We would look our best and add value to the salon with more services.

One day, I looked around to see other people in my shop making more money than me.

They were the women cutting and styling hair—the hairdressers.

I went home and chatted to my mum about it. I was working so hard, but I was not making enough money for my goals. And this motivated me.

I wanted the fast track. I wanted to put my hard work into a career path that would get me a better return.

So I kept talking and talking about hairdressing.

Then, my mum said yes.

"If you are serious about this, you can do it," she said. "But you have to go to Ho Chi Minh City. They have the best training courses. You can learn to be the best hairdresser from the best teachers and set yourself apart from everyone else."

The same principle of sending me to the gymnastics school to become a national champion: Go to where the best trainers were, the best teachers, the best coaches. But once again, it meant leaving and being alone in another city.

By them, we were very poor, and things were different from when I left to do gymnastics.

People needed to go to Ho Chi Minh City to study because Hanoi was poor and the teaching was not as good, so they accepted a lower standard of hairdressing. Whenever money was an issue, it was easier to take the simple way out. Charge less, and do a lesser job.

My mum saw the future. She knew, based on my dreams, I would need something more.

At work one day, my mum had a meeting with my boss, telling her I wanted to be a hairdresser.

"When she comes back from Ho Chi Minh City, when she is qualified, she will still work here with you. This will build your business and be a standout from everyone else who is just self-taught or trained in this town. You will have something that sets you apart."

I thought this was a great offer, and I was excited to hear my boss' reaction.

The boss said ... no!

She did not believe in me the way my mother did. She knew what she knew, and that was working with local clients, with local girls trained locally. No big changes. Nothing had ever changed in her life. So she kept doing what worked for her, safely, and in her own way.

And her way of dealing with it was to reject the possibility of change.

This was what she said about me to my mother:

"Your daughter cannot be successful at hairdressing. She only knows how to do pedicures."

Of course, because I worked so hard, she made a lot of money from me, so she wanted me to stay exactly where I was.

She did not want to lose me with my focusing on something else. She also didn't want to lose me to another business.

Her world was all about controlling the girls who worked for her, and this would keep them at a level of skill everyone was comfortable at. No one got too far ahead, and no one left if they were not successful enough to go to work for someone else, or try to start a business for themselves.

By know, you probably know my mum is where I had gotten my determination from. So she talked to my boss.

And she told her the same thing: No.

This was the mistake of telling my mother I could not be successful.

After all of the successes in my life, the discipline and the dedication to perfection, she knew what I could achieve.

My mother believed in me. She knew I could do anything I said I would do, and do it better than anyone else.

So I became determined. I stomped up and down in our home, furious at the woman who was trying to hold me back, furious she would try to convince my mother of a lie

But it was okay. My mother believed in me. She calmed me down, looked me in the eyes, and told me to listen to her.

She said, "If you want to go, go."

So I left to study in Ho Chi Minh City. At first, I was just studying, and there was so much to learn.

After focusing down at the feet and the fingers for so long, I now had a whole new world of beauty to focus on.

And very quickly I learned to love it. The colours, the styles, the personalization. And there was so much money to be made with extra services, extra products, cutting, lengthening, extensions, hairpieces.

And after I started learning, I would keep going back to Hanoi to work. I went back and used my new skills in my old boss' business. I committed to work there, not just for the money, but also out of respect for her giving me the job straight out of school. I also knew she trusted me and I appreciated the responsibility she gave me.

I had also brought in a lot of money in the past, and now I was more valuable.

Sometimes I did nails, sometimes I was asked to cut and style hair. It didn't matter to me. I did everything. I worked harder, because I could do more. I was in demand. I was learning, and working, and gaining valuable experience.

Being a beauty therapist is not a glamorous job.

For anyone believing it looks like the advertisements on the billboards and in the hotel spas, here is a reality check.

Let me share how I started my days.

Have you ever heard that one of the keys to success of a business is "Location, Location, Location?"

The salon was close to a public toilet.

Every morning, I arrived early, and people were going to the toilet, even without the doors being open—just on the wall, or wherever they felt like it. Then they would sit out the front of the salon, in the way of my getting the salon ready. I would have to tell them to get up, to shoo them out of the way.

Nobody likes to see people sleeping out the front of the business they are going to spend money in. And they don't want it smelling like the toilet!

I had to clean it all, hosing down the wall, freshening up the area. I had to get the salon looking attractive for the wealthy Hanoi clients who would use our services and give me tips and help me in my future goals.

I went beyond the basics and over-delivered in my role of a store manager.

After cleaning outside, I would go in and wash my boss' clothes from the day before.

Then I would go and buy her coffee and breakfast and two cigarettes.

And I did this with my own money. I did all of this as a part of my job. I invested in my own future.

I considered this the price of my apprenticeship. It was

important to separate myself from everyone else, to do what they did not do. I continued to learn from my boss. It was important to keep her happy so I could learn how to run a salon, because I didn't plan to stay there forever. I planned to start a business for myself. For now, though, I kept learning hairdressing and practicing in the salon what I had learnt.

My boss loved me. I was bringing in so much business, making her famous, and I was also refining my skills as well as learning how to run a business.

I worked with her for just one more year, when the opportunity to start my own business came.

I opened my first salon when I was still 19 years old.

I was very proud of myself. I was a highly skilled, hardworking beauty and hairdressing service provider. And I was ready to take over the world.

But if you were there and looked at my shop ... I have to be honest. If you were walking past, it wasn't very impressive. The shop was just fifteen square meters—the size of a small bedroom.

Really small.

Okay, I have to go one step further. It was not a shop on the walking street or the main road. It did not even have a front door. It was a room in the walkway in front of a supermarket. I set up at 14 Nguyễn Văn Tố then in the Hang Da Market nearby.

Now I know it does not sound very exciting, but you have to remember I was just nineteen years old. I was in charge of my own life. I was able to do everything myself. And I knew this was just the beginning.

I did not take clients from my old boss. Instead, I started with a totally cold market. I had to smile and talk to the people walking past. I had to encourage them to come in. No walls, no hiding, no privacy. Sales became my responsibility as well as doing the work of the hairdresser.

But it was great. I had done my training, and now I was free to be in business for myself and in control my destiny.

I created my first brand, Hai Yen. And when I moved into the next phase, my brand was YEN TRANG - and became famous throughout Vietnam. If your mother wanted a great hairdresser in the 1990's it was probably at this brand name salon.

But for history, here are some of my early addresses in the centre of Hanoi.

50 Quán Sứ
29 Hà Trung
55 Cửa Nam
32 Hàng Than

I worked hard. For years and years. I kept moving into bigger and bigger salons. Then I opened more salons, and after ten years in hairdressing and beauty, I was very famous in Hanoi.

I did have very successful salons. Yen Trang was a household name in the celebrity and A-list of society in Hanoi. I made a lot of money and employed a lot of staff.

Then I decided, if I wanted to be more famous and more successful, I would have to build my personal brand. My name needed to be bigger. I wanted to be famous and successful.

My childhood was still driving me, and my time of being so poor with my mother was pushing me

So I started expanding. My salons got bigger, we got more staff, and we found new ways to make money.

Now, I was doing all the thinking for the salons. People go away to learn about hairdressing, but not about business.

It was important for my staff see the difference between what we did and what everyone else did. I wanted a more entrepreneurial staff so everyone made more money.

In the early days, hairdressing salons only used to wash and cut hair.

There were no products, no shampoos, no conditioners, no waxes, gels or hair sprays. No product sales. It was hard to make money this way.The typical haircut would make us two dollars, just from the sale of the haircut service. That was all. It took a lot of haircuts to buy a new house, or car, or even new clothes.

So I sat down one day and I did the maths.

I sold a sample of a new product for curly hair for four dollars.

Now, I cut hair for a one dollar profit and sell one bottle to get five dollars.

I did very well, finding great products and bringing them in. At the wholesale rate, I had great margins. And with many stores, I could get volume discounts.

I trained my staff to sell.

We would make a seventy percent profit from the sale of products and add-on services. I would even help my staff to make more bonuses and tips—a happy customer tips more than one who gets ordinary service. And people love being offered extra things to buy.

We became a one-stop beauty shop, and our haircuts were talked about in the city as being one-of-a-kind.

Want a foot massage with your haircut? Add another dollar. A facial before the cut? Another two dollars.

Buy some shampoo and conditioner to take home? Another four dollars.

Everything added up, yet there was no system, and if I

wasn't there, the system could break down. Staff just don't think the same as a business owner.

When I was small, it was very easy: Treat everyone like family.

When I was bigger, I needed to treat it more like a business, become more formal in my process. But I had never run a business this way.

I focused on my skills in the services I provided. Learning and sharing the trends in fashion, hair, and beauty.

I always thought I needed to go far away to learn, so every month, I flew to Ho Chi Minh City to learn more.

To get something new to show off in Hanoi.
New ideas in beauty and hairdressing.
A fresh perspective on the industry and the business.

I was always the first in Hanoi with new things, new styles. Regular travel away from my business helped me to build my skills, and working on my business from the outside in helped me to build my salon with new systems, as well as cutting and colouring ideas and styles.

Then my life changed in a big way. In 1999, I had my first overseas trip to Germany and its hairdressing convention.

It was my first time overseas and it opened my eyes to a whole new world. I saw the vision of my future in this industry and to be number one, I had to keep innovating. My clients wanted to see the styles and designs in hairdressing from around the world. And I would bring them to me.

I had started my education in hairdressing going to Ho Chi Minh City. Then things had changed for me, and now every year, I took overseas trips to discover new trends and changes in hair and beauty.

I believe my success came from my vision on how to create amazing results for my clients in Vietnam. I was doing what no one else was because they were afraid to try new things. I had no fear like this. I knew if I helped my clients, my business would grow.

I was successful, because I saw what my clients wanted and I found it for them.

I was successful, because I trained my staff to provide excellent service, and under my personal brand, clients knew the standard they would receive.

I saw it, what I wanted to achieve.
I did the actions needed to get there.

Even then, I understood the principle of result and action. Create a desired result, then put the action steps into place to get there.

I wanted to be a leader in the beauty industry, so I continued to do things differently from my competitors by traveling, and by learning and sharing it with my staff and my clients when I returned.
Every time I traveled, I learned something new.
What I did was amazing in my salons, because everyone else was so far behind me. I set the trends in Vietnam by following the trends of Europe.

But after ten years of growth, my business hit a road block.

When I stopped to look at my business, I saw there were problems.

I had a lot of salons in locations around the city.
I had a lot of staff.
My brand was based on my personality and my standards, but this was the 1990s. Not much internet, no good communication between salons.
I could not be everywhere so I was trusting the systems of the business to work. My system was quite simple and

ineffective: I hired people, trained them, and then hoped they followed the rules.

Quality control was difficult.

Managing people and treating them as staff was difficult. I wanted everyone to be nice and to feel a part of my family, but it was hard to discipline or fire your family.

Managing the cash flow of the businesses was hard. All of our business was cash and we had no tracking for the product sales or knowing what might have been stolen. I didn't even know if some people were being given special rates.

Going overseas, I bought better systems for tracking finances, including point of sale equipment. I found software for booking appointments and took advice from other salon owners about staff management systems with rostering and scheduling. Plus, I took classes on management and leadership.

Our next successful phase after Germany was from 2000-2006.

By now, I was in every five-star Hanoi hotel with a salon. Hotels like:

Daewoo
Sofitel
Melia
Hilton

I was famous on TV as an entrepreneur and a business success. A business leader. People wanted to know how I built my business.

I was famous in magazines because we did the hair for celebrities, famous women and actors and actresses.

If I was going to do advertising, I would be spending $5000 for my brand name. I did not know how effective it would be because people already knew me. Spending money in this way didn't make any sense. But if I rented a salon in a five-star hotel, everyone came to me. They could find me and have the treatment or haircut they wanted.

So I didn't need to advertise; instead, I just put my salon in the best hotels and people flooded in the doors.

At that time, there were fewer than ten five-star hotels in Hanoi, and I was in all of them.

The high standard was to match the high price people paid to stay in these hotels. People paid a lot and expected a great location, and great treatment.

My clients stayed at the hotel and used the services because I was there. Sometimes it was the wife of a traveling businessman. Sometimes it was a businesswoman who was in town for just one day. The hotel was a great location.

High-profile clients like celebrities, actors, and politicians liked going to the five-star hotels.

Now, I'm training around the world. I wanted to train people around the world, teach people how to make more money in their salons.

It was never just about haircuts.

Mindset

The mindset for success

Everything matters. How you think—think too small, and you achieve very little; think too big, and you might create unrealistic expectations. Get it right, though, make it motivating, and you can achieve anything.

I have always been a big thinker, but not in the way you might think.

My life, my goals, the world around me have given me challenges. It has always been frustrating for me to look at the world and see what was possible. Most of my thinking was negative. I always saw the negative side of a situation. I always thought about why things didn't happen the way I wanted, and I always thought I might be missing out on one opportunity by doing something else.

So I was always looking over my shoulder and around the room in meetings in case something better was waiting for me. I had to keep watching out for it. I couldn't miss out.

For example:

If I was spending some time with a friend or a business colleague, even if the experience was good, I had something in the back of my mind. I would always be asking myself questions: Why is this meeting happening? How did it come to be important? Why am I here? What am I getting from it? What else could I be doing?

So it was a huge case of "overthinking!" And it was exhausting.

Overthinking

When we overthink, we get caught inside our heads.

When we are stuck inside our heads, we fail to see what is going on around us, which means we miss out on many opportunities because of focusing internally and not looking out to see the amazing things waiting for us.

When in meetings, we might not even hear what is going on with the people in the meeting. The conversation we are having with ourselves dominates.

What else happens when we overthink?

We stop. We do not take action.

When we think too much about the consequences of a decision, we don't make that decision.

When we think too much about the negative possibilities of a deal, we don't do the deal.

When we think about the best case/worst case scenario for long enough, it all gets too hard.

Overthinking causes paralysis.

And this paralysis makes it hard to get any sort of momentum and drive toward our goals.

We get frozen in time, and we keep things exactly the way they are right now.

We can also be labeled as introverted, eccentric, or strange. People meeting us for the first time, doing a deal, making business connections, may see us as too conservative.

None of this matters if we are in a position of strength and power. But we can have a problem when meeting people for the first time and we are just beginning to build our business.

I go out to work and earn money, but I don't trust other people. I worry they will steal from me. And I worry my business will fail. So this creates an environment where a lot of people have a negative approach or opinion of me.

If my salon opened in a new hotel or on a new street, then I created instant competition.

If someone opened a salon near me, then they needed to steal my customers to get them. My customers love me and the way I do business.

So my competitors had to talk bad about me to get my customers; be negative to me to steal mine. And this makes me trust other business people less and less.

And this was when I was in my twenties, in the early days of my business.

Belief and trust

If I look back at my young self, I realize I had lost belief in people.People in general had proven they could not be trusted.

I didn't believe in love, because my parents broke up.

I didn't believe business partners would help, because my own father's business went broke.

That meant I was cynical and doubted everything around me. Sometimes, I wanted to like people and trust them, but to protect myself, I had to go back inside and not reach out.

But one day, I lost belief in myself. This was a horrible period of my life. I had trusted myself and believed in myself all this time, then suddenly, it was gone.

This was the hardest thing, because I needed to believe in myself. It was how I got motivated. Even my negative mindset about other people was not stopping my business from growing.

If someone else had an opinion about me, it did not bother me. Even the closest people may have a bad opinion of me. It was okay, though, because I could always trust myself.

But if I looked down on myself, then I had a problem.

My first failures were giving me self-doubt. I had not created the everlasting success and financial security I desired.

When I looked at this time in my life I saw that my motivation was all wrong. My focus was wrong. And my attitude needed some adjustment.

Until my first failure, I didn't realize the importance of attitude.

If I didn't learn how to have good attitude, I would have more of these moments of self-doubt.

If I did not build my self-esteem in those early days, I would not have had such a great business growth, because I proved to my clients and my staff that I knew our path. I had goals. And they came with me on the journey.

But my lack of belief in other people was beginning to isolate me. I could not trust, and it always came back to my youth. My injury. My parents breaking up. And being poor.

In the past, I thought about why many of my staff did not listen to me. Many would leave and go work somewhere else. Others would start a business in competition with me.

I would have negative thoughts, self-talk that was not productive.

"I'm not good enough."
"I didn't help them enough."
"I didn't take care of them."
"Why don't they like me anymore?"

I had forgotten the lessons from my mother about compassion and selfless giving. I had become selfish and assumed everyone would be with me forever. I thought I was their mother. Their mentor.

I wanted them to work hard for my goals like I had worked hard for my boss.

I never thought to stop and consider maybe they had their own goals and their own dreams.

Mentors

The best relationship is with someone wiser than you

I have spent a long time working on myself. Personal development is what I know now; it is how I have always lived my life. Every step of the way I needed to take charge of my own life.

From the age of six, I was independent.

This meant I had to develop my strength. My resilience. Learn lessons quickly in order to be successful, or fall behind and fail.

I have always had a hunger for learning to be the best, and I looked to my teachers, my coaches, and my parents for the fastest way to master something.Many times it was simply spending the time and having the discipline to work on what I needed to do, again and again.

For example, during gymnastics practice, many of my peers complained about the schedule—they didn't like the early mornings; they didn't like the diet; they didn't like the constant stretching and exercise; and they didn't like learning the beam, the bars. They wanted to have fun.

But I knew in order to win, I had to do what my coaches told me to, and to do it better than everyone else.

So I didn't complain.

Complaining never achieves anything.If we complain, it does not help us to learn.

If we complain, we only hurt ourselves.

So I always looked for ways to improve, even if it meant a lot of work. In fact, I have to be honest: doing more work made me happy, because I knew my peers and competitors would not want to do it.It was easier for me to be better than they were, because I did the work.

From a very early age, I had the discipline.
I was my own mentor.

And I won the medals. Led the class. Stood out from the crowd.

In my younger years, the people influencing me had always been in positions of authority. I trusted them. And listening to those I trusted helped me to become successful in my professional sports career.

After gymnastics, and working in fashion, hairdressing, and five-star hotels, and even beginning in network marketing, I was my own mentor.

Listening only to myself created a level of success, but it also had its limitations.

Instead of listening to other successful people, I would learn by watching them, reading books, and attending training workshops.

But I never had a private mentor or a coach.

I never had that one special person whom I trusted implicitly to share with me their wisdom and experience so I could grow professionally and personally.

It took more than twenty-four years of traditional business, its ups and downs, its successes and failures to finally listen to someone who could tell me the facts for a happy life.

And I had to be at my lowest point to finally listen.

I told you I would share how I turned my life around from

struggle to freedom.

From having no choices to having total control of my choices.

My mentor helped me to look back over how I had lived my life, how I had run my business, and here are the things I learned:

In the first twenty-four years of being in business, I had gone bankrupt five times. More than most people will ever experience in their entire lifetime.

Every time, I learned something new, but I could not create the life of freedom I dreamed of and craved with my soul.

I hope you can learn from me, and not make the same mistakes.

People management

In the early days of starting my hairdressing salons, I was working from a very small shop.

When I was working by myself, alone, running the business was easy.

Selling services was easy. Selling products, getting repeat business; these things I understood.

I knew that, to get my customers back, I needed to give them a great experience.

Then, I began to grow.

I moved into a larger premises, and I started to hire staff.

But all I knew about business was doing nails and hairdressing, and selling and making customers happy.

I made my staff follow what I was doing, and I helped them to become good at one particular area: nails, or hair, or facials, or massage.

For a while, the business grew.

But managing people was hard work.

I had no systems in place for managing people. No process for hiring or firing. I was a softie and found it hard to give feedback, hard to discipline others the way I had disciplined myself.

I was frustrated by the lack of communication with my staff and why they didn't understand how to do business my way.

So I restricted them, gave them just enough to do their jobs but no more.

My mentor showed me how I had failed in responsible managing. All I did was try to keep growing.

I had always focused just on the technical side of the business.

He educated me in the way of the "E-Myth" by Michael Gerber.

In that book they talked about exactly my situation.

I was a great technician and a good salesperson, too, but my ability to perform beauty therapies was my top priority so customers would come back again and again and bring in their friends. I focused on this exclusively.

Get a customer. Make them happy. Get them to rebook. Ask them to tell their friends.

I built my business quickly this way. Unfortunately, my lessons were in the area of human resources or staff management.

Richard Branson from Virgin Group said that every employer should focus on their staff first, customers second. Without happy staff, you cannot have happy customers.

I was trying to make my customers happy, but I did not focus on my staff.

So I lost a lot of staff, since I did not support any of their dreams and goals and they chose to seek other places to achieve them.

Some of this came from the fear of training up a staff member, only for them to open in competition with me down the road.

I took this personally, but never spent the time investing in my staff.

I was tough on them, kept them busy so they couldn't leave.

Investing in my staff was something I did not do. I kept their skill level just high enough to make my own business successful, but not enough for them to start their own businesses.

If I had taught more than just the technical aspects, I might have had a more successful business from the start. The best staff have the most skills, not just one or two.

If you can do massage as well as nails as well as hairdressing, you are a more valuable staff member. But I was afraid they would leave, so I only gave them one skill.

If you can manage money well, do product ordering and stocking and merchandising, you are a more valuable staff member. But I only kept my staff busy on their service delivery and working with clients.

I realized many years later that my staff had decided to leave me because they thought (and they were right) that I did not care about them. History repeated itself—I was the same as my old boss.

The customer was everything.

And so was my ego. Having a successful salon. Being popular with my clients.

And becoming rich.

I did not care about my staff.

This is one of my greatest regrets from that time in my life.

So my E-Myth moment came not with just one salon, but with many.

I was running from salon to salon, trying to keep up the quality of service, trying to meet every key client and celebrity and have them like me so they would continue to come back.

The staff were never empowered to have the same level of relationship, so they felt unloved and uncared for. And eventually most of them left.

Some even directly sabotaged the business—stealing equipment, supplies, and even customers when they opened in competition.

I never looked at myself.
I just blamed them.

I never realized what I should have done to look after them.

My mentor taught me how I had destroyed my own business by not caring for the people who made it successful. He shared ways to build a team, how to lead it, and how to grow it.

Looking back, it made so much sense. And with my mentor's help, I could forgive myself for the mistakes I had made, and look to the future, knowing I would not repeat them.

But my second big failure in life helped me to learn another lesson.

Control

I have been what many people call a "control freak" for my whole life. I like to be in charge, and in control. I was always responsible for myself at school and at home, and when I began working at seventeen, I had to be in control, so I have always been used to directing my life and making things go in the direction I wanted them to.

This is easy in a controlled environment, of course. My first work was in a small salon. My first business was in a tiny store. Even when I grew with a limited number of staff, I could control most things.

My mentor took the time to share with me that I was not invincible. I was not a superwoman. Not everything was under my control. He had to work around my huge ego and my control issues to make me see how my second business failure had occurred.

We could not control the weather. I agreed.
We could not control how people fell in love. I agreed.
We could not control a plane as a passenger. I agreed.

So it should make sense when you see where my failure had occurred.

I had spent years building up my businesses from small salons to now having a national brand.

I was a BIG brand—my name, my face, was everywhere. Because I had a successful brand, it was time to not just be a local success, but to really maximize the financial potential.

So I expanded into the high-class end of town.

I began running beauty salons in five-star hotels deliberately. The women who wanted my services would make their husbands stay in these hotels. The men who wanted their women happy would book these hotels.

This was great business for the hotels, as they had a

drawing card for the customers, and it was good for me because I could charge top dollar for the services I had previously done much cheaper.

Money was coming in, and I was seeing the future brightly.

I was a national celebrity, and the movie stars, politicians' wives, and A-list people were coming to me to have their beauty needs met.

It was a great time.

Until 2003.

SARS

Severe acute respiratory syndrome (SARS) is a viral respiratory illness caused by a coronavirus called SARS-associated coronavirus (SARS-CoV). SARS was first reported in Asia in February, 2003. Over the next few months, the illness spread to more than two dozen countries in North America, South America, Europe, and Asia, before the SARS global outbreak of 2003 was contained.

According to the World Health Organization (WHO), a total of 8,098 people worldwide became sick with SARS during the 2003 outbreak. Of these, 774 died. In the United States, only eight people had laboratory evidence of SARS-CoV infection. All of these people had traveled to other parts of the world with SARS. SARS did not spread more widely in the community in the United States.

When SARS arrived in Asia, it was like the world had stopped.

Our salons had no business for six months, but we still had our rent in the five-star hotels.

No one travelled; they all stayed home.

Everyone was afraid of SARS becoming an epidemic that would kill everyone, like the black plague. The media made a big deal about it, but as you can read above, it was really blown out of proportion. Only 774 people died out of the worldwide population of more than six billion.

But you cannot be logical with a potential epidemic.

No one was going out in public, and if they went anywhere it was with a face mask and sanitizing gels, and they never engaged with anyone.

No one visited salons because it had close contact with other people and was seen as a high-risk activity.

No one spent any money. No one cared about anything more than just staying alive, and when people moved into this frame of mind, I learned something.

I could not control people who were emotional and afraid.

No amount of logic would get people to hop on a plane with other potentially infected humans and risk their life, just to have a haircut.

Even when the outbreak was contained, it took another six months for business to return to previous levels. But by then, I was broke.

All those hotels, all those overheads, all those bills, all the staff pay. It added up, and with no income, we had to close the businesses.

It was a terrible time.

My mentor helped me to look back to see that SARS was beyond my control.

Irrational and emotional people cannot be controlled with logic.

And a high-overhead, high-risk business relying on travelers, the profits would always be hard to control.

I look back now, and while SARS was bad luck, it did teach me a lot more. If I wanted to have financial freedom, I needed more control. So eliminating businesses with too many factors beyond my control helped my financial position.

It took a few years to rebuild, but I did. Nothing stops me.

My mentor taught me about financial risk management with my next business failure.

World Trade Organization

In 2007, the best news we got in Vietnam was the green light to welcome investment into the country through the WTO.

"Vietnam's accession to the WTO in 2007 undoubtedly offers foreign investors greater access to various local business sectors. Vietnam has made commitments in 11 service sectors (110 sub-sectors). Except for a limited number of sectors designated as unbound (such as secondary education or machinery and equipment renting/leasing) or restricted (such as the banking sector or electronic games business), most service sectors are currently open to full foreign investment."

This was a time to look at Vietnam as a growth market for international brands.

There would be big investments by foreign companies, and big risks by local business owners wanting to work with those companies and set up their brands in the marketplace.

The Vietnamese currency was floated, and Vietnam Dong was devalued to make it cheaper to bring in the other brands. The slide began in 2007, then over the next ten years, it lost fifty percent of its value against the USD and other currencies.

The currency failed. The experiment didn't work at all. It made it cheaper to visit Vietnam, but more expensive for Vietnamese people to buy anything from overseas, including all of the business deals linked to the value of the Euro, not the Dong.

With my history in beauty and my regular travels to

Europe, I did some deals. At the time of the WTO announcements, I was finalizing some great opportunities, and within a short period, I controlled seven big international brands. Plus, I locked in the rights to manage these brands throughout Vietnam.

All beauty and hair products I owned the rights to.

But when I look back, I was not in control of finance. I was so caught up in the "fever" of international brands, to support my business and meet the responsibilities of my agreement, I had failed to realize the impact of poor financial decisions.

I had locked in my deals in Euros.The effect of currency being floated and allowed to follow market trends and free market factors was beyond my control.

The currency dropped and dropped—from 16,000 Dong to the USD to 17,000, and then to 18,000. Every day I woke up, my products were costing more to import. But my customers had no extra money, so my margins were getting thinner.

I was making less money.

And then I was losing money.

I had debt in Euro increasing day by day until it had gotten to the breaking point. I had to reneg on my agreements, close my import business, and I had to look at new opportunities.

If I had had a mentor, I might have seen the risks, and maybe not have ventured into such a volatile business deal.

If I had looked objectively, I would have seen there was only one winner: the Europeans. The Euro was already eight years old, and it was stable. The deal with the WTO and Vietnam was not good for our country, and many businesses collapsed as a result.

My mentor reminded me that financial education would have helped, but it may not have stopped me if I was headstrong and determined to try to make money from this opportunity that was promoted around the country as a good thing.

Not long after this, my next business learning experience occurred.

And unlike SARS, this had a major impact on the entire country and Asian region.

The GFC (Global Financial Crisis)

I had just bought a franchise from the UK to get back into hairdressing to help me to dominate the market.

The product licensing had not worked for me, so I thought a proven business model would be better.

I still didn't have good financial advice, and the Vietnamese currency was still devaluing, week by week.

So (and this may be a surprise to you) I bought a franchise from the United Kingdom, which was in British pounds, the strongest currency in the world at that time.

It was to be the master franchisee for Toni & Guy in Vietnam. Already they were forty years in the market, and the chance to be the first with such an innovative concept was too good for me to resist.

Here was how they marketed the idea of having a franchise:

"TONI&GUY is seeking motivated, business-savvy individuals with a background in the hairdressing industry who are looking to join a brand synonymous with quality, fashion, and heritage. Becoming a TONI&GUY Salon owner comes with many perks, including built-in support systems and a rich, inclusive culture. We would love for you to partner in our mission to upgrade the industry through spreading the TONI&GUY standard of quality from coast to coast. Become part of a legacy; Become part of the TONI&GUY family."

"The TONI&GUY strategy is based on simplicity: an easy-to-follow business model with a proven operating system and world-class educational system.

"Our goal is simple: We provide each client with a highly

educated hair stylist who can make them look good and feel good. We establish relationships with satisfied clients who return often and recommend us to friends and family.

"Our revenue model is based on providing clients with price points that fit every budget. We want to be a salon for the entire family. We focus on multiple touch points throughout the client visit to enhance their experience, with an emphasis on educating the client on how to maintain or reproduce the look at home, including prescribing tools and products for use.

"Our staffing model is primarily based around salon-ready graduates from our TONI&GUY Hairdressing Academies, as well as a simple but quality training program which attracts non-TONI&GUY graduates.

"Our goal is to open salons within close proximity to our TONI&GUY Hairdressing Academies, allowing for a mutually beneficial and proven successful relationship.

"TONI&GUY Hairdressing Academies supply our salons with industry-leading graduates who are looking for a career with our brand. In turn, the academies provide career diversity to our salon teams with the opportunity to become academy educators. The Advanced Education course schedule offered alongside the basic program gives both salon team members and academy faculty the chance to progress their skill set. The perfect win-win situation!

From www.toniguyfranchise.com

I was blinded by my own ambition

All the warning signs were there of me repeating my mistakes. But I could not see them.

The UK currency was set for the fees for purchasing the rights and paying franchise fees.

A struggling Vietnamese economy making every British pound cost more in local currency.

The Asian crisis of the GFC, with people losing money in

investments, property, stocks, currency, and more.

Plus, I had no franchise experience. My own salons had always fallen to me as the front person, the leader, the face of the business.

Now I had to rely on the support of an international brand and trust that it would be marketed well enough in Vietnam for me to make it work.

It didn't.

I lost hundreds of thousands of dollars.

Sometimes, I think I am being tested with how much I need to learn before I find my true success.

But I did find out a lot about myself in this time.

I realized I loved to focus on the best things in life—the salons in the five-star hotels, the international brands, and the hairdressing franchise.

I realized that having a five-star lifestyle business had higher risks, and that I was the person responsible.

I realized that international business in this form needed a specific set of knowledge—currency markets, franchising fees and rules, importing and duties and taxes.

I was never good at this, and the results showed up in my eventual failure.

So I thought it was time to look at doing something new.

And this was when I looked at network marketing seriously for the first time.

Network Marketing

My mentor taught me a lot about this industry, one I had a few years' experience with before I met him. My first experience did not work, and it nearly cost me my life.

In 2006, I had started working with some products

featuring the juice of the Tahitian Noni plant. I had the salons, and a great database of customers to promote it to.

While other businesses were failing around me, I was lucky enough to have worked out how network marketing could work. In 2007, I earned over one million dollars in commission.

I took a risk and set up a company as the director of a new company who wanted to do business in Vietnam. Due to the local laws, the USA company owners could not be the directors.

I trusted them.

I believed in them.

So I put my reputation on the line.

Some of the leaders from that company visited Vietnam a lot. There were lots of big meetings, and everyone made lots of money. Locals were being paid a lot, but the big leaders would fly in, hold a motivational style event, then leave.

I was travelling to the USA, attending conferences as I was making money in Asia.

But at the same time there were serious health issues with the rest of my family. My mother, my father, and my own health all started to take the centre stage and demand my attention.

I focused on my business so much, it hurt those around me, and while I made money, I was ignoring them, building the business, and managing the company's obligations.

I was not even looking when, overnight, the company had decided to close. They simply packed up the office and left. They still owed money and products to thousands of people, but the company did nothing to support the market or my country. They just abandoned it—the company, the other leaders, everyone.

And all responsibility for the company's obligations to the government was left in my hands to solve, because I was the director.

People were complaining to the government, and the government was asking me for answers.This was so dangerous for me because of the emotional reactions of all of the distributors for the company. They could not find anyone else to get angry at, so they got angry at me.

Enough so, I needed to have police for protection to stop the distributors from knocking on the door and demanding I pay them back.

There was over $100,000 in taxes and fines to be paid, and I had to pay it personally or be put in jail. I couldn't help my family if I was in jail. So I had to pay it.

The problem with this situation was emotion combined with traditional thinking—when people are in pain and someone offers a solution in writing, they believe it.

People believe things if it is in the newspaper. In writing.

So the press wrote bad things about me, and people believed them.

And the company made no statements to support me; they just abandoned me as they had abandoned Vietnam.

The press got hold of the story and were promoting that, as the directo had all of the money. The statement from the US owner had more credibility than me. People trusted an overseas businessman who had run away more than the word of a woman who had risked her reputation and exposed herself to financial ruin.

In the end, it destroyed my reputation in Hanoi businesses and in the local community.

And it taught me a lot. I learn along the way, and I never forget.

My mentor asked me what I would do differently, and I said that I would not risk my reputation for a company who was too afraid to do it themselves. I had worked so hard and had no spare time, so I had money but no time, and my health was suffering.

So I moved to Ho Chi Minh City and started a new life.

I changed my name.

Irene Hoang was born.

A new business came to me at the right time: At the lowest point in my life, lying in a hospital bed halfway around the world, with my life falling apart all around me.

But there was a determination in my attitude, even at that time.

After everything I had gone through, I still believed good things would happen.

I wanted to see long-term success for myself and my family.

I learned the two keys to retiring:

1. A company needs to have longevity to offer true passive income. You cannot make lifetime retirement income with a get-rich-quick plan.
2. You can retire if you have a system, because it will allow you to let the system do the work while you live your life.

Choosing the right mentor, the right sponsor, is important. When you, in turn, bring people into your business, there is a key point.

You don't need to teach them; you need to lead them.

You need to have a vision and the right attitude to help them.

And most importantly, you need to care for people, because this will help you to support them even when you don't feel like it.

My mentor's results inspired me when we were talking, and I joined him. He had learned a lot about life and business while travelling the world, and because I was ready to listen, he shared his secrets with me.

I always choose to learn more in my life; I never assume I know everything.

It might come in the form of a book, a training, or a teacher.

This time, it was a mentor who I could follow, because he had what I wanted.

He told me I needed to be hungry for money, and hungry to help people, and hungry for the freedom in three areas at the same time.

- Health
- Time
- Money

So I followed his advice, and I proved I could do it. (In a later chapter, I will talk more about being hungry for money and how powerful that can be.)

So what was the difference between me and other people? After all of my failures and all of the experiences that would stop most people and have them give up?

Despite all the challenges,
All the problems,
All the haters,
All the negative feedback; and
All the things that stop most people because it is all too hard.

**I want this book to show you
that it doesn't have to stop you.**

My mentor inspired me to think big, to have a big goal. And my goal now?

To be number one, worldwide. A leader who has created

success for millions of others.

So, because of my passion, I am again working towards this goal.

How have I changed in the last five years?

1. Personal Growth - I have grown throughout this process. Now, I've made bigger goal to grow more to achieve my new goals.
2. Discipline - I stick to a plan to reach my goals I had set and follow the system that has proved effective.
3. Willingness to work hard - I needed a new plan to reach my new goal because it was so much bigger than what I had already achieved.
4. Supporting and edifying my upline and downline - We must edify one another to positively impact the business.

I had made the switch from working on just money goals, to working toward success in three areas:

Health freedom
Time freedom
Money freedom
All at the same time - in equal measure.

After focusing 100% on money for so long, I had no family time and was so sick I nearly died.

My mentor taught me about living a happy life. How it would change the way I spent my days and nights, change the way I looked at business, and change the way I thought about success.

When I learned this philosophy, I agreed with it 100%.

My mentor asked, "If you have money but no time, are you happy?"

I said, "No."

"If you have time but no money, are you happy?"

Again, I said, "No."

"What if you have your health but no money, are you happy?"

I shook my head.

"So if you have any one of these three things, without the other two, you cannot be truly happy. If we work to achieve holistic happiness, we will have all three things in balance. When the balance is right, we can increase the happiness level and have freedom."

"Okay," I said. "Please show me how."

Then he began helping me to understand even more about what makes an unhappy life.

For example: you might be the fittest and healthiest person on the planet, but have no money. Instead, you spend all of your time exercising and planning your diet, so you are out of balance. Your health is great, but you don't have any money for travel, entertainment, or to treat your family.

Or, you may spend all of your time working, like I did. Then you have no time, but lots of money. Without time, you can't have happiness, which is time with the ones you love and a healthy body to enjoy that time to its fullest.

Or, you spend your time being busy, but not focused in the right way. So you are busy, but do not make enough money to justify your actions, and the wrong actions lead to a failure to reach your goal.

$X = Y$

Action = Results

I always chose action. Being busy. Working hard. Making the most of my time to work on bringing in money.

I chose hairdressing and beauty, which required long hours.

I chose companies that wanted to come to Asia, brought in their products and spent all of my time promoting, marketing, and selling.

I chose network marketing companies for their vision., but I didn't realize they did not always match my vision to create the success I wanted.

My mentor reminded me that we often work-work-work, doing lots of actions, but we don't really know where we want to go. What is the final result?

X = Y
Action = Results

I needed to choose the results first.

This was a total reversal of the philosophy I had lived by my whole life.

I saw an opportunity and worked hard to make it successful, which it always did. But it never lasted.

My mentor told me to start with the end in mind.

Where do I want to be?
What do I want my life to look like?
How do I want to spend my days?
Who do I want to spend time with and enjoy my life?
Where do I want to live?
What car do I want to drive?
Who did I want to have on my list of friends?

I had always thought it was enough to have a logical strategy and plan for my actions, but I never reached my goal of financial freedom, and I never reached time freedom, and I nearly died.

My mentor reminded me to work backwards.

I saw his results: his Lamborghini, his Bentley; all

outward signs of financial freedom.

He is now retired and does not actively work in the business. His system is working. He has time freedom.

And he has health freedom. His health is the best it has ever been because he has time to ensure he gets everything he needs to help his body perform at its optimum level.

So I choose action, and I get results.
This is a logical strategy that makes sense to me.
So I think: if he can do it, I can do it.

I saw everything he was doing and I knew I could also create the same freedoms.

If I did the same actions, I knew I could have the same results.

I could model from him.
I could learn from him.
I could follow the system.

Before, my focus was centered on money.
Then I moved to a family center and set my goals to serve my family.
Now I understand the last part.

If I want 100% HAPPINESS, I need:

Financial freedom
Time freedom
Health freedom

So happiness is the ultimate goal. All three aspects of life in balance and harmony.

We should choose the results we want, then take the right actions. How do we do that?

My mentor said we follow a system, which would get us the freedom we desire.

I saw the system was working.
I saw it got him amazing results.

I saw what I had to do to get the same results.

So I took my mentor aside.

I looked him in the eyes and said, "I want to learn from you.
Exactly what you did, I will do, too, so I can get exactly your results.
Not fifty percent of the results; one hundred percent and more. I want to be even more successful.
I want to be the biggest and best in my country.
And after I achieve this, I want to be the biggest in the world."

I knew no one could grow their business faster than I could grow my own.

Because my system was there. I knew the goal and the result and the outcome of the system.
And anyone can follow these actions to get the same results if they copy the right things, and if they stop doing actions that got them bad results in their past.

Some thinking had to change.
Some processes and systems did not work.

So of course, I asked my mentor: "Why didn't I find someone like you a few years ago?"

Timing is everything, though. I had to be ready to listen at the right time.

But the KEY is in CHOOSING.

Finally, after twenty-four years, I chose.

The right choices will create the right results which create the actions to make them come to reality.

For twenty-four years, I chose many different methods of action and had hoped for a result.

By the end of all of it, I had nothing. But I had taken a lot of action. This just shows I was taking the wrong kinds of actions. Action itself is part of the plan.

There is no benefit to looking at the past, unless we learn from it and change our actions in line with our new goals and dreams. Then we need a new type of action to achieve them.

Now I choose happiness as my ultimate goal and result. This makes my actions clear and defined and easy to duplicate.

I needed to work with a company that could give me every chance to achieve health, time, and financial freedom. Working in partnership.

I needed a mentor and a sponsor who could help me; they needed to have done it and to be able to show me the way. Working in partnership, so I then could become a mentor to my team and the next generation of networkers.

I have a family to care for, and money helps to do that. I have a young daughter who wants me to spend time with her, and I need time to do that.

People who don't want to work this hard toward a worthy goal are selfish. They aren't thinking about the extra people in their family. You can't stop, and you don't have enough unless you can care for everyone around you. This is why I work hard, but I work to create happiness. No longer do I work just to work. No longer do I work long hours just to prove I can. I do not hurt my body; I nurture it.

So now I work, not for now, but for the next life—when I am gone and my children and family need me the most.

I can look back on the last few years, knowing I did everything to achieve a balanced, successful, happy life. And I have it now.

And through the rest of this book, I will show you how you can, too.

Be a mentor to yourself and others

Any job I've had I followed because of my passion.

I love helping people.

I love to help men and women in my country gain confidence in their life, to be bold and brave and have the courage to start in business and chase down their dreams.

I have always led the way as a supporter of women in business.

The best business for women has been network marketing and direct sales, because there is no barrier to entry and no gender bias, just equal opportunity.

So I take the time now to mentor women who come to me wanting a happy life. I take the time to show them, by example, exactly what to do and how to do it.

I have them shadow me and follow every step I take.

Why is this so important for me to do?

In the early days of my life, I had no mentor. I drove things myself. Followed my own vision and trained myself, taught myself, mentored myself.

I lived and directed my path with just my vision and my experience. Of course, a lot of this experience turned sour. I did not always do it right. But I had no one to ask. No one gave me any shortcuts to success. Most people saw me as a competitor. And I did not realize the secret was to find a mentor and ask them for help.

Now, I have mentors everywhere in my life, and I know what I need to work hard on. And most importantly, I mentor myself every day.

I sit down and have a conversation about what results I want for the day, and I motivate myself to take the necessary action.

It's not about money, but the health, time and financial

freedom I desire.

The turning point was finding a mentor, whom I have mentioned throughout this book. Life changed 180 degrees when I started to listen to him and demand that he share his secrets with me.

Choose the mentor you want in a particular area of life and use them until you don't need them anymore. I still go to my mentor today, but as an equal, not as a student. I have transformed into the mentor to my team—I have become my mentor.

Right now, I am grooming people in my team to be leaders, so they can have the balanced and successful happy life.

All I do is lead, mentor, and pass the torch to the next generation to do the same.

I am my greatest mentor, because I was given the tools to lead myself, teach myself, and learn from myself.

Health Freedom

Freedom to live at 100%

When I look back on the decisions I made about how I spent my time, I can see how they affected my health.

My mentor made me take a serious look at the way I had treated my body when I was young. He reminded me how I was lucky to have a chance now to live well and live a healthy and happy life.

But it was not always this way. I have been very sick twice in my life, and it looked like it would end with me young and unhappy.

My focus was always on action, getting things done to achieve my goals. Every day I focused on specific habits, actions, and disciplines to get ahead, and my body at its best helped to make my business a success. Back then, I was building a personal brand and an international reputation, and I needed my body to serve me to get me through the long days.

So I worked hard, and I pushed my body very hard.

But your body will tell you if you are not in balance, and it will give you a wake-up call you can choose to listen to or to ignore.

After ten years of working in my salon, I was just thirty years old, but I started to feel my health suffering. My staff were noticing. My friends were noticing. My husband was telling me to go to the hospital.

The wake-up call

I didn't listen to my body until one day I was so sick, I was sent to the hospital.

They said I had a stress-related problem where my hormones were affecting me like I was twenty years older.

The doctors told me that the stress in my work was affecting the ability of my body to monitor my cortisol levels.

"We have learned that cortisol levels are crucial to maintaining the body functioning well and is a key factor in regulating ALL other hormones. If cortisol levels are not where they should be, estrogen, progesterone, testosterone, human growth hormone, and thyroid hormone cannot perform their functions well.

"The medical community is well aware that high stress and anxiety are killers and are the most common causes of premature aging." – The Wellington Institute.

They tried to explain it to me this way, but I didn't understand. The language of doctors can be confusing, long complex terms and conditions. I needed a simpler explanation.

So they put a mirror up to my face. Now I could see what they were talking about.

I looked so old.

The stress and the lifestyle was making me old before my time. I was thirty years old, yet I looked like I was in my fifties.

The naturally occurring human growth hormone in my body was not functioning right. Nothing was working right. My hormones were destroying my body because I was out of balance.

I was stressed and aging prematurely.

It was a sign of something I had to pay attention to right away.

My voice was changing—I would be speaking and suddenly lose my voice. Other times, it boomed; and still other times it whispered.

My memory was playing tricks on me.

My weight started to go up and down without control.

My bones were aching and hurting and stopping me from sleeping.

It was a scary time.

The doctors were not very positive in their prognosis. They said, "Maybe you won't live to see forty years old.

"If you can't control the stress hormones, it will ruin your body; you will be taken over by the hormones, and your body will be out of control and you'll die."

This was the worst news a mother could hear. No one ever wants to die while their children are still young. And they were so young, it broke my heart.

No one wants to be given an end date for their life. It is the fastest way to let go of caring.

So I had to get my stress under control—eat better, exercise—but a part of my brain has given up.

One of the problems of being diagnosed with something that might affect your life in the short-term is that no one wants to give you insurance.

When the doctors said I might not live long, I could not get life insurance, even in my early thirties. I was too much of a risk for the companies who said they were there to take care of you when you were sick.

I was such a liability for an insurance company; they believed the doctors and expected me to die.

How could I fight and win when everyone was against me? They wanted me to suffer and die. But this motivated me more. And the more I focused on being successful, the more my health improved.

I did not have the option to insure my death, so I just assumed I was going to die soon.

And if I was going to die, I might as well work hard and make as much money as I could, while I could.

Old habits

So I did the only thing I knew how to do.

I worked hard. What was making me look older and telling me I should change my focus, I ignored at that time. Instead, I chose to work harder.

My mindset was to focus on my family. I had lived as a person in a rich family and a poor family. I did not want that for my own family. I wanted my family to have choices.

Even if I was dead by the time I was forty, I wanted them to be financially setup.

I was scared people would look at me like I was poor, a terrible feeling with my mother when I was a teenager.

I was scared of going back to that—so scared. I could not do it to my own family and I could not leave them behind without some security.

So I focused on making money for a higher purpose.

I was determined—my family must be rich, not poor. This drove me toward my goal. It became my single focus. Nothing else mattered. If I died tomorrow, my family must be taken care of.

And even though my health was suffering, an interesting thing happened.

It was not what you would expect, and it changed my mind about the power of goals and singular focus.

When I focused on making money to support my family, I made money.

And like magic, my health started to improve.

I could really build my businesses fast and bring in a lot of money. I could quickly meet the goals I had set, because I had a series of goals that were bigger the longer I worked, to provide a level of comfort and support to my family.

I had highs and lows, and not every business decision worked, but the size of my businesses grew. The money flowed in. And I felt good.

Because I did not feel sick anymore, I did not focus on it at all. I did not give the sickness or the disease any power over me.

This is a mindset that would ultimately affect every area of my life.

My belief? If I have money, I have everything and I can take care of my health. Because it is up to me to make my life work.

No one else will be responsible for me.

No one else will pay my bills.

No one will care for my mother and my father, or my two sons.

So I worked day and night, day and night. Most people would have given up, said to themselves there was no point and just enjoy their last days, been with their family.

My work ethic, though, was getting me through this time.

Work, Work, Work

Because of my stubbornness and determination, I was successful. I would win this battle and create financial security for my family before I die.

I was not paying too much attention to the facts. As each year went by, I was still alive. Long after everyone thought I would be dead, I was still going. And getting stronger, and faster, and more successful.

So what is the advice I give to you, reading my book? About how to deal with people who write off your life as being over?

Prove to yourself and prove to them you can do it.

My philosophy in health and in business is this: Left or Right?

If everybody is turning right, I will turn left. And I will be alone without competition and make a success for myself.

People said, "What if you turn left? Would you die? Isn't it safer to turn right with everyone and stay a part of the crowd? Follow the safe advice? Stick with the crowd?"

Well then, I must have died many times, because I always make the decision to go in the other direction from the masses. I choose the opposite path to the one taken by thousands before me. I choose the path most people do not want to take. I choose to be brave. I choose to make my own destiny, not follow and hope it unfolds.

"Wait! I am still alive!"
Maybe my method works just fine.

My philosophy is to go in the opposite direction of the crowd, and in the freedom of this space, you feel good. And if you feel good, then you do everything better, faster, and with more energy and more determination.

Logic says to go the safe way. To be like others. To follow. But other people's logic does not work for me.

If I am using logic, I do not feel good. In using my intuition, working on solutions and opportunities that feel good, I succeed.

My intuition tells me that when I work, I will create something better.

My intuition tells me when I work hard, I will set an example.

And after a while, my intuition tells me this hard work is making me healthy again.

So I defied the health predictions of the doctors, and the insurance company, and even friends and family who believed I would die.

Now, seventeen years after they said I should be dead, I am happier and healthier than ever.

What changed in my health?

With the intensity of the goal I had set—providing financial freedom for my family in the event of my death—I worked hard.

I had laser focus in the direction I was going. And as I worked harder, I began to look after my body. I began to combine exercise with my phone calls. I walked on a treadmill while I worked out my meeting schedules. I supplemented my diet and kept my levels of nutrition high.

I put the same level of energy into managing my nutrition and exercise. I knew if I focused on making money, I would make money. So I focused on improving my health, and it got better, too.

In time my life moved forward and the greatest miracle occurred for me. I had a baby girl.

She is the love of my life, my motivation for working and building my business and keeping healthy. She takes a lot of energy to keep up with, so I work hard, stay fit and eat well so I can love her and be active with her.

Now, I can look back after all of the challenges and truly say I have proven everyone wrong.

But mostly I can say I have proven myself right. I knew I could do it. From a near-death experience, to the most happy and successful I have ever been.

I was able to give my family everything they needed to support them whether or not I was here. But because I am here, I get the best of both worlds.

Because I focused on my health, it has given me the freedom to live an exciting life, travel the world, and be there with my family. This leads me to the key to getting the most out of every day.

How did I get control of my time?

Time Freedom

The most valuable thing you cannot hold on to.

What do we have a limited amount of?

What can we not control, slipping away from us?

What is the one thing we all want more of?

What is the fastest thing to disappear?

Who is the master of us all?

What is invisible, but all-powerful?

Time.

Time is what we use as a benchmark when we look back.

It is where we go to look at the mistakes we have made. We go back to a previous time in our lives when we made a decision or took a particular action.

It is where we create dreams, goals, and possibilities. But the past can color the future with fears and anxiety.

Time.

When we realize we have a limited amount of time, we begin to make decisions and make things happen.

What are our choices for spending our time?

Being an employee

Do we want to exchange our time in a job? Are we happy to spend our time traveling an hour to work each day?

Spending eight hours sitting at a windowless desk, staring at a computer screen, working on someone else's dream?

Do we want to climb the corporate ladder and be a manager of people who resent us for our achievement? Do we want to spend each day dealing with the politics of happy and unhappy people who want our job or want one even better?

Do we have the energy to deal with the petty issues of those who do not want to be told how to work and when to have their vacation? Managing people can become a lot of work!

Do we want to be a salesperson always having to get one more sale to make money? If we do not go to work, we can not make sales. And if we do not make sales, we do not make money.

Do we want to be a shop assistant, waiting for customers to come in every day? We have to be patient, keep the store clean, stack the shelves and answer questions, hoping people will buy something. Are we in a business where the products make us excited to talk about them? Do we have a personal story about those products? How they changed our lives?

Do we want the following challenges of exchanging our time for money in a job?

- Traffic
- Boss
- Managers
- No control
- Few holidays
- Restrictions on relationships
- Travel, but not where you want
- Breaks when you are told
- Working in a structure with people you did not choose

What are some other challenges of working in a job?

- Limited income potential
- Agreed timelines on pay increases
- Taxation
- Asked to do extra hours for free or minimal pay increase
- Asked to work with people you actively do not like
- Asked to do things you do not agree with
- Asked to compromise your integrity
- Asked to compromise your ethics
- Covering for other staff when they are sick
- Have to justify when you get sick
- Have to ask for vacation time
- Have to work when children are on vacation
- Have to work while the rest of the family goes on vacation

Why do people do it?

All of the decisions we make are based on a combination of logic and emotion—about one percent logic and ninety-nine percent emotion for most people, because emotions are much more powerful.

Emotions control us because our feelings affect our physiology and our mindset.

Emotions drive our spontaneous and impulsive decisions.

Emotions that keep us safe are stronger than those that might put us in danger.

So here are some situations where key emotions and feelings keep us from changing:

- Safety
- Security
- Consistency

- Repetition
- Habitual behaviors
- Low-risk
- Being loved
- Not being alone
- Being cared for
- Having enough money to survive
- Having a standard of living we can adjust to
- Having people around us who are predictable
- Having someone responsible for us
- Not making our own decisions

These are much stronger in their ability to influence us. Staying the same is easier than change.

Look at the exciting emotions and feelings in situations we describe as:

- Risky
- Passionate
- Daring
- Dangerous
- Adventurous
- Entrepreneurial
- Working for yourself
- Working in another country
- Having staff of your own
- Having a team reporting to you
- Selling on commission only
- Direct Sales
- Leadership roles
- Investing

Can you see why being in a job fits this type of mindset?

There is no risk in continuing the way things are, according to the person who is focused on staying the same. Of course, this assumes that things will never change in the job.

Most people do not think that far into the future, because the future's uncertainty scares them.

Self-Employed

The next dream many people have is to be self-employed, to be their own boss.

In this way, the work still exchanges time for money, but the business activities generate money.

For example a consultant charges $300/hr and needs to bill "X" number of hours to meet the expenses of having an office, business stationery, costs of delivering the service, and so on.

Or a traveling hairdresser visits offices and charges per haircut, but they have no salon or staff, they just work by themselves, carrying with them the tools of their trade and their skills.

The self-employed person has to find clients, provide great service, and keep people happy to have repeat business and enjoy the freedom of not having a boss.

Many people like this idea of managing their own time. Don't want to work today? Just don't go anywhere. Of course, this can be irresponsible and affect existing clients and work relationships.

What are the emotional drivers linked to being self-employed?

The first is freedom. Work when you want, if you want, with whom you want.

What others?

- Set your own holidays
- Set your own rates for products and services
- Sell the products you love
- Sell your time

- Be the expert in a topic or an area of study
- Choose your own vacation time
- Work the hours you like
- Choose to keep or lose clients if you don't like them
- Choose the suppliers and other service providers you work with
- Work from home
- Work from an office
- Work from airports
- Work from anywhere in the world (if you have a product or service you can sell online or have clients anywhere)

The challenges this career lifestyle has?

- You don't work, you don't get paid
- Clients are hard work to keep
- Clients are harder to find in the first place
- Individuals can be squeezed out by big corporates on price and range of service
- Self-employed people may have taxation issues. (because they are often treated like companies, but don't get all of the benefits or legal protection)
- No safety net if you fail
- One bad client or review can create a ripple effect throughout your business, especially with social media and ratings systems

Being self-employed does not provide time freedom, but it does provide some freedoms.

Having a business

When we have a business, we have a new range of responsibilities.

We may have staff, inventory, insurances, company obligations, and taxation rules to follow.

There can be offices, warehouses, factories, retail stores, and other rented premises.

There is a board of directors and the need for meeting after meeting.

Often there are fees to pay. For example, franchises, business licenses, international banking, levies and taxes, and more.

When we have a business, we may have to learn new things. Our stress may rise trying to manage and maintain all of these new factors.

Many business owners like the level of detail required to manage all of these things. Why? Because there are many benefits to having a business.

A business should live a life separate to the founder or owner. It has a purpose to make money through the sale of products and services, but it also should use more than just the time and energy of the founder or boss.

With a business, the owner or creator fills it with their energy and passion, and this energy is given to the team running the day-to-day business. In a perfect world, they carry out the vision of the founder.

What are some of the other benefits to having a business?

- You can create a system or way of running the company so anyone can step in and take a role to make it work.
- You can duplicate a concept like a retail store or a consulting service, grow more locations and hire more people.
- You can multiply your income through the work done by other people.
- You can walk away from the business, or even sell it

for a profit and start again. Or start something totally different. Or retire.

What are the challenges?

- Most businesses take two to five years of solid work to get to the point where they can run without close management.
- Staff never believe in the business as much as the owner. Most are self-centered and think more about vacations, pay raise, promotion, and their own goals.
- Breakdowns and economic circumstances beyond our control can affect the business. For example, running a lighting business in a town where they have a lot of blackouts.
- The owner holds responsibility for legal issues.
- The owner holds responsibility for accidents involving staff members.
- The owner still has the responsibility to ensure everyone gets paid, even when there is a cash flow problem.

So owning a business requires substantial capital, reserves, financial management skills, risk management, human resource management, marketing skills, sales expertise, and more.

Not everyone has these skills. And even fewer have the cash.

So they stick to being self-employed and contracting themselves to other businesses.

And we have seen those challenges.

So what else is there?

Investor

An investor sees employees, self-employed people, and businesses, and wants them all.

They want them in cash-producing assets, businesses and concepts that generate positive results.

They do this by investing their capital in those areas they like. They do not spend time themselves in all of the business roles we have looked at so far.

They invest in a business that can make money, leverage their capital to help it expand and grow. Consequently, they get a return each month or each year to repay their investment and provide ongoing cash flow.

They invest in ideas, and bring people together into this cash-producing machine, the asset.

They have the ability to invest in idea after idea, business after business, asset after asset, and this generates multiple sources of positive cash flow.

And they can see cash flowing in from all of their businesses in many different ways. From when they were young, it was from ice cream sales in the summertime.

When they started running businesses, they had always thought of making money. So often they let others make the mistakes in the bad ideas to help them spot the good ideas.

They focused on the positive cash generation of the businesses they invested their time and money into.

Investors look at their future as a series of cash investments into people, of cash invested into ideas, of cash invested into ongoing businesses and systems and modes of doing business that generate positive cash flow.

Because of the limited number of hours in the day, they know they must make good decisions. Then they let go and let other people carry them out. They watch it grow, and only intervene if absolutely necessary if their cash flow dries up.

They do not invest just in a person; they invest in a person with an idea of systematically making money.

They do not invest in a business; they invest in a solution to a business problem or a personal problem, and they let the systems and the people work to solve those problems.

Investors stop exchanging time for money.
They let money work for them in a systematic way.

They exchange money for proven results, and they know the more money they put in, the more they get out, because assets provide money out in the form of positive cash flow. Every dollar they put in, dollars come out the other end.

This leads to a unique level of experience. Because they are not focused on the day-to-day activities, they see the results from a safe distance. They cannot be caught up in the emotions of the day-to-day staffing issues and power struggles. Instead, they can see the results.

They can see the result of a bad decision in staff turnover.

They can see the result of a bad company investment in the lower dividend.

They can see the results of a bad economic climate in the shrinking of a division or the removal of a product line.

But they see it all in numbers and figures and in spreadsheets, and in reports and meetings.

They get the top level information at a meeting, while the reports give the details.

They get the big picture from the CEO, while the numbers tell the financial truth.

They can remove the emotion from doing business by focusing on the "business" portion of a business.

When a person starts to think like an investor, they change. Instead of focusing on the microlevel of day-to-day activities, they look at the big picture, monitor how the business runs.

Instead of looking down at their desktop at numbers, they can look out across their factory and see harmony or discord.

Instead of staring at one person being interviewed for the job, they can meet everyone at the Christmas party and learn everything they need to know about the culture created in the company.

The best part of having this attitude about money means you no longer are exchanging anything for time.

The best thing about thinking like an investor is not looking where to spend your time, but looking how to invest wisely for a good return.

You are thinking of the result you want, then taking the relevant action.

If you continue to repeat actions that hope to get you where you want to be, you are thinking like an employee hoping for a raise.

If you repeat actions to show how good you are at what you do, you are thinking like someone who is self-employed.

If you have a good idea you want to make money from and leverage your time through products and services, you are thinking like a business owner.

And if you are thinking about how to get the best possible return on investment of your intellectual, financial, and emotional capital, you are thinking like an investor.

**Think of the result you want.
Then start taking the action to get it.**

Some people go a long way into their life before they realize the path they'd first taken did not give them they wanted. I had taken twenty-four years.

And I didn't want to take it any longer.

Now it's time for you to take action to get control of your time, so you will have time freedom.

Let's make some money—big money.

Financial Freedom

Financial Freedom

My mentor asked me if I wanted the secret to wealth and financial freedom. Of course I said yes. I needed to understand this secret.

When I put the secret to the test, I became financially independent in three years.
I made One Million Dollars in just seven months.
And I secured my families future.

He said passive income is the secret to wealth.

Anything else is working too hard, and will eventually mean we have to sacrifice either our time or our health to make money.

I will show you a few examples so you can see ways you can take advantage of this and leave yourself with the time and health to enjoy your money.

Passive income is the key to giving you financial freedom. This allows you to decide when and where you do whatever you want.

Let's look at your current lifestyle.

This is the measure of the quality of life you have, based on the available cash you have; how much you can spend, and how much freedom or restriction you have.

If you only have $1,000 a month in income—the average for many Southeast Asian and Eastern European countries—you probably spend it all every month.

It is not enough to get ahead; in fact, you may not even have enough left at the end of the month for any sort of entertainment or enjoyment, and definitely none for travel.

I know you get caught in the cycle of trying to make enough money to pay your bills, your rent, and to put food on the table. I have been there just like you.

I have sat with just a few hundred dollars, wondering how to buy clothes for my children, how to get medicine for my mother.

It is a terrible feeling.

If you have $2,000 a month in income but a $3,000 a month lifestyle, after one year you probably have $12,000 in debt. After three or four years, you might have a serious situation where the interest alone on your credit cards would be killing you. When you live beyond your means, it is a high-stress lifestyle.

When you are in this kind of debt, you can never have the financial freedom you desire. You are always chasing to meet your payments on your bills and your debt.

What about a more positive situation?

If you have $5,000 a month in income and only $3,000 in expenses, you have a positive cash flow position. You are working full-time, and maybe even have two jobs. You don't have any spare time, but you do have the income to provide some security for the family you never see.

You can quickly pay off any debts. This is good. By maintaining that hardworking lifestyle, you could save money for buying a house, investing, or traveling and buying some luxuries.

When you have $20,000 a month in income and $10,000 a month in expenses, you have raised your quality of living.

You should also have more money for saving and investing.

If you get to $50,000 a month in income, you could say you are rich or even financially free. But if you have to work every day to make that kind of money? What if it takes twelve to sixteen hours per day, and you never see your family and run your health into the ground? Is it worth it?

This is what happened to me.

And this is a part of why I am writing this book for you.

It doesn't matter how much money you make if you sacrifice your health and your time. Then, you get to the end of your life sick, tired, and alone. And earlier than you had wanted.

This is why the key is to have passive income.

Passive Income Ideas

By choosing the right sources of passive income, you can invest your time in the way that you want to. Passive income is a way of buying back more time. So many opportunities out there to make money exist, so I want you to open your mind to all of the possibilities. Passive income is that cash flow that comes into your life every month, whether you are personally working or not.

It has some key principles:

1. Letting go of working too hard
2. Having a system that generates income
3. Having the discipline to let the system do the work

People have gotten more and more creative with how they make money from existing assets and resources. Plus, the internet connects us all faster than ever before to learn new ways to make money.

Let's look at a few ways.

Real estate

More and more people with homes are now using sites like Airbnb to rent a room or their entire property. This is using a combination of active and passive income—you promote the property on a shared online platform, then you receive payments for people staying in your home.

In the traditional real estate investment, you buy a home or an apartment and rent it out for one month or one year at a time.

Each month, you can make an income while you just keep the property in good order. You pay your financial obligations of mortgage, rates, and other outgoings of the property, and the cash flow helps to cover those costs and make a positive cash flow.

Other people buy new apartments in a big complex, saving money on the initial price, then wait for the value to go up and sell for capital gain. The cash flow is less frequent than renting out but it may make a ten, twenty, thirty percent or more return in just one or two years.

Investing in the stock market

With the internet connecting the world 24/7/365, it is possible to trade stocks and shares on multiple markets around the world at any moment.

Trading is quite an active process, while simple investment in the market for the long-term can provide passive income.

With low-risk "blue-chip" stocks, people can build a portfolio worth tens or hundreds of thousands of dollars and receive monthly or annual returns in the form of dividends, as well as capital gains when they sell the stocks at some point in the future.

Of course, not all stocks go up in value, so it can be seen

as a higher risk strategy.

Trading in foreign exchange markets is a much more active trading investment strategy, and it relies more on research and following trends in that industry. Most people prefer to be passive investors and just use an experienced broker or trader to do the active part of the income generation.

Dividend income is a dividend paid to stock shareholders in the form of cash in your bank account. Dividend-paying stocks are especially enticing for those wanting to make a living with passive income, as they will get payouts each quarter or so. Even Warren Buffet, historically, is a fan of dividend-paying stocks. If you are going to go this route, make sure you educate yourself and pick solid stocks so you can depend on your dividend income for years to come.

Being an author

Once the initial work of creating a book is done, you can sell it online. And in paperback and audio formats, you access the growing education market. You need to develop an effective marketing plan, but selling books can be a great way to produce passive income. Once your book is available on a site like Amazon, you could receive money each month for doing absolutely nothing. Obviously, the more time you spend marketing your books, the more money you'll make.

Not everyone is able to be a movie star, getting a percentage of gross takings like Tom Cruise does, but even TV stars can get ongoing passive income from shows that are seen for years and even decades later, like Seinfeld.

Create a Mobile App

If you are a bit tech-savvy and can come up with some unique ideas for mobile apps, or improve upon an existing app, you may land yourself a great source of passive income. Every app on your phone is making money for somebody, somewhere. For instance, Joel Comm made over one million dollars from his iFart app. We won't even talk about the ridiculous money that Angry Birds brought in. While those are the exceptions, there are plenty of people making thousands of dollars per month with their mobile apps.

Create an Online Store with Drop Shipping

With the explosion of e-commerce, drop shipping has become very popular. Here's how it works: you create an online store that offers products from certain manufacturers. A person visits your site, orders a product, and your system sends the order to the specific manufacturer. The manufacturer then completes the order by shipping it directly to the customer. One of the cool things about this type of business is that you do NOT need to order inventory. The customer pays for the product, you collect the profits, and the manufacturer stores and ships the products to the customer. It's as simple as that.

Buy a Vending Machine Business

A successful vending machine business can be a great way to make passive income. The key is to find the right places to install your vending machines. Check with small businesses that have over 100 workers in the building on a daily basis and see if they have need for vending machines. Ask those workers what items they prefer to have in the vending machine and then stock accordingly. Once again, if you want to reduce the amount of time you are involved, consider hiring someone to stock the machines for you, then get more businesses and factories.

Start a Business and Have Someone Else Run it

Owning a business can be a good passive income source, provided you've got the right people running the business for you. Purchase an existing business, or open a new business and leave it in good management hands. Your great business idea can be a viable source of passive income.

Rent Your Car for Ad Space

How would you like to make money just for driving your car and not have to pick up any passengers? By allowing companies to place advertisements on your car windows, you can earn a few hundred dollars each month simply by driving your car around town. Check out Free Car Media to see how you might be able to make passive income by wrapping your car with an advertisement.

Buy an Existing Online Business

The beauty of an online business is that most will allow you to work from anywhere. Starting one from scratch can take a lot of time and resources. Why not consider buying an already established online business? There are hundreds of online business listings for sale in varying price ranges. Check to see if there is an online business for sale in line with your passions or hobbies, because if you are going to be working, why not do something you actually enjoy doing?

Buy a Laundromat

Here's another turnkey passive income business idea. Many cities have established laundromats available for sale. Here is how it would work: You buy the already existing business, make sure you have someone to manage the day-to-day operations, and then "soak up" the profits.

Open a High-Yield Account

Looking for a low-risk way to make passive income? Then look at opening a high-yield checking, savings, or money market account. The yields are much higher than most local banks but still come with insurance. While this won't make you filthy rich, it will be a safer way to make consistent income and not lose your money.

Rent Your Stuff

Thousands of people every day are looking to rent any variety of items. Craigslist can be a great place to advertise your items for rent. Here are some ideas of products you could rent out: extension ladders, party tents, tables and chairs, utility trailers, log splitters, chainsaws, snowmobiles, and ATVs. You can even rent out your car when you are not using it.

Create an Online Course

Online courses can be a great source of passive income. Here's how they work: You create a value-packed online course that helps solve a problem or fills a need. This course can include videos, e-books, and emails with pertinent information. Customers sign up to purchase the course, and your system automatically emails them everything they need to access the materials.

What about me?

As you can see, there are a lot of ways you can make passive income. Hopefully, this list has helped you to narrow down which source of income is best for you. So, if you're tired of the traditional way of making money, implement a few of the passive income strategies above so you can start working less and making more money while you sleep today.

The key is to realize you cannot work forever.

If you work hard but have no time, you are not free.

If you don't work hard and have active income, you are not free.

If you work hard and get sick, you are not free.

You have to look at other options.

Let's have a look at how we can understand why many people get stuck working on active income and never truly get the freedom passive income provides.

I want to quote Robert Kiyosaki and his book "Cashflow Quadrant." This is a life-changing concept, and as a bestselling book, it changed the mindset of millions of people around the world.

If you understand it, you will realize why making money is easy, but making passive income takes a strategic approach and a desire to be free.

In Robert Kiyosaki's words:

"There was an important diagram my rich dad showed me when I was a little boy. It was a diagram known as the Cash Flow Quadrant. And the Quadrant is made of four different people who make up the business world.

"So my rich dad said, 'In the business world, there are Es, and E stands for employees. And the employees, you can always tell who they are by their core values. An employee with the president, the generator of the company, will always say the same words. The words are, "I'm looking for a safe, secure job with benefits." That's what makes them employees because their core value is security.

'The other one of the four is the S for the small business owner or the self-employed and again their core values will cause them to use the same words which are, "If you want it done right, do it by yourself." S means they are also solo. Generally one person act, they operate by themselves.'"

The Cash Flow Quadrant

_"On the right side of the Cash Flow Quadrant are the Bs. And my rich dad said, 'The B stood for big business, or like Bill Gates. For Bs define big business as 500 employees or more. And their words are different.

They'll say, "I'm looking for good system, good network, and the smartest people I know to help run my business." Unlike the S, they don't want to run the company by themselves. They want smart people run the company for them.

'And then, the fourth of the Cash Flow Quadrant is the I. And the I stands for the investor. These are people who have money work hard for them. These people in the B Quadrant have people work hard for them. And these people in the E & S Quadrant are the people who work hard for the rich here in the right side of the Cash Flow Quadrant, for the Bs and Is.'"

"So, early on in my life it was my poor dad who always said to me, 'You know, Robert, go to school, get a high paying job...' And so my poor dad's core value was to be an employee. He wanted a job security, promotions, steady paycheck and all these.

"And so it was my rich dad who said to me, 'You know, Robert, if you really want to be rich, learn to build businesses.' It made more sense to him to work hard to build a business. Something you own, and something you pass on from generation to generation to your kids.

"Whereas my poor dad said, 'Work hard...' my rich dad said, 'Why would you work hard for something you'll never own, and you can get fired from it right away?' Again, that was the difference of values.

So my rich dad suggested I learn how to be a business owner and learn how to be an investor. And that's where the big difference is. On the left side of the Cash Flow Quadrant, these people work for security, they work for money also.

"On the right side of the Cash flow Quadrant are the B and I peoples' key value, what they want is freedom, financial liberty. They don't want to have to work in a job any more. They don't want to have to work for the rest of their lives.

"So the beauty of building a business and learning how to invest is very simply that this is passive income.

You work hard for a few years and possibly for the rest of your life, that passive income keeps flowing to you."

This Cash Flow Quadrant applies to network marketing as a method for passive income. Robert Kiyosaki explains why:

"I'm often asked why I recommend multilevel marketing, especially when I'm not in network marketing business myself.

I'm like many people. Early on, I had a very negative or close-minded attitude toward network marketing system.

But I've changed my mind. I've opened up the way to think, and I looked into the network marketing industry.

And I found some things that are extremely beneficial, especially for those people who look for changes from E and S to B and I in the Cash Flow Quadrant.

Communications and sales skills are essential for somebody in the B Quadrant. And network marketing companies, not all of them but some of them, have excellent training programs that will teach you how to sell, how to communicate, how to build businesses...

Many people would not go to the B Quadrant because they are afraid of rejection. Network marketing teaches you how to handle your own fears, fear of rejection, and build that self-confidence. That's essential for the B Quadrant."

~ Robert Kiyosaki ~
Reproduced from The Cashflow Quadrant, available at Amazon.com

Now let me share with you how I apply massive action to achieve financial freedom with passive income, because I have chosen my path to passive income with network marketing and have broken sales records, built a team of more than 150,000 people around the world, and am the most successful networker in my country.

It is a concept I call:

"Hungry Money"

My overall philosophy is to work hard for what I want. Because I know what I want. I am very clear and have laser focus.

My motivation has always been my family. Learning from my past, I can take the lessons and apply them now to any project and see the action I must take to get what I want.

This layers my experience from every successful time in my business career, one on top of the other, until I have hundreds of layers of knowledge and wisdom. I can pull any layer out at any time to show myself what to do in that moment.

Some people have said I work like a man. Maybe the drive, the energy, the focus is what they see. They only have to ask me why I work so hard and they would see the woman and mother behind the engine room of my success.

I found the best way to be successful is to simplify the business you are doing and get energetic about achieving your goals. Without this, we get bogged down in details and confuse ourselves.

I want to tell you about hungry money.

This is the money you know you need so you do not go hungry.

It is the money you have to make so your expenses are paid and you can enjoy your life.

But most importantly, it is the money you make because you are hungry.

What things can you be hungry for?

When I had my first business failure, I was hungry for food. Things had gone so bad for me and my family, there was nothing. So I had two choices.

Choice number one: Rely on other people to give me

charity. To take welfare, unemployment benefits, receive secondhand clothes from people, and receive food donations.

There is nothing wrong with this, and for many people, it can help in the short-term.

Choice number two: Get back to work.

This has always been the choice I take because I always desire more. I have a passion to achieve. And I remember the days when we were all hungry, and I know I do not want to go back there again.

Choice number two helps every time there is a challenge or a setback. I know that by getting back to work, working for hungry money, I can create what my family needs.

Because one thing is very important here.

My family is large. I have a lot of people to feed. Yes, I take the responsibility to feed my children, my parents, my extended family, and more.

I have to house them and to provide them with the enjoyments of life. So when I say I have a challenge, it is ten to twenty times bigger than most people's challenges. It's for a lot of people, never just for myself.

What does that mean?

It means my challenge is to create a million-dollar business, not a small business.

I do not just need to make a few thousand dollars to buy food and clothing. Again, I have an extended family who count on me. I need more—much more.

So hungry money is the direct result of my searching for million-dollar opportunities, for multi-million dollar companies to work with, successful people to partner with.

Because I think about the big numbers I need to meet my goals and take care of my family.

The work I do means any challenges I have are just

numbers to be achieved; simple mathematical equations that show me what I need to achieve and make it clear just how hard I must strategize. Plus, they tell me where I need to spend my time to get the highest return, and what to avoid in the way of distractions and low-yield activities.

Of course, there is a mix of risk and stone-cold sober judgment and strategy involved. Nothing great was ever achieved sitting at home wishing and hoping and avoiding the risks of the real world.

I have always taken the road less traveled and turned left when others turned right. I do what others will not. This is the key to having a successful business, in my opinion. I can be focused and have the best of both worlds.

Let me ask you a question.

How hungry are you?

Are you so hungry, you can't remember the last meal you ate?

Are you so hungry, the bills you have are crushing you from above?

Are you so hungry, your credit cards look like a millionaire but in the negative?

Are you so hungry, travel for you means knowing how long it takes to walk somewhere/catch the bus?

Are you so hungry, the world is only seen on Google Earth?

Are you so hungry, the passion and life has been squashed out of you?

You have to take control. You have to get up now!

Hungry money means setting a goal.

It is about knowing what you want and then magnifying it so big and so compelling, it calls you like a giant magnet. It pulls you toward it so strongly.

Wanting to make an extra $100 so you can buy a dress isn't going to be hungry money. It is just a convenient "want."

Wanting to clear your $10,000 credit card isn't hungry money. That is just solving a short-term problem cramping your freedom.

Buying a Lamborghini with cash for $300,000 needs hungry money.

Living in the best neighbourhood and in a three million dollar house requires hungry money.

Flying first class uses hungry money.

Wanting to have a nine-course meal on the top of the Shangri-La Hotel in Hong Kong will need hungry money.

Wanting to stay in a hotel suite for a week at $2000 a night costs hungry money.

No one else will give you the things you want. You have to do it.

Hungry money needs three things:

1. A goal that drives you
2. An attitude that says nothing will stop you
3. A vehicle to get to the goal

Having the goal is okay, but without the second and third parts, it does not do anything.

Having the attitude only is not enough.

Having a vehicle, without goals or attitude, is nothing.

This is how you make the hungry money of a visionary entrepreneur.

My mentor gave me the tools and unlocked the motivation to create the kind of money I needed. After twenty-four years in business, in so many different businesses all around the world, what I had was right in front of me at home in Vietnam.

And he reminds me that the opportunity was there, but I made it happen now because the timing was right and I was ready.

I brought every part of me into this business and applied everything I know. Sometimes, it just takes someone to guide us toward the direction we need to go. I talked about my mentor throughout this book, and now you know why I am so grateful.

Now I have passive income, and I am mentoring others to have the same by following their intuition, following my plan of action, and following my system.

The student has become the teacher, and I am enjoying every moment.

Quotes

"What doesn't kill me makes me stronger."
Irene Hoang

"If you think you cannot do, you give up.
If you think you can, you do."
Irene Hoang

"Life and
Happiness
Are all a choice."
Irene Hoang

"The bigger your goals are, the bigger a problem it takes to stop you."
Irene Hoang

"Clarity leads the way to success."
Caroline Rochon
Success University for Women

"She stood in the storm, and when the wind did not blow her way, she adjusted her sails."
Elizabeth Edwards

"Purpose and energy fuel success."
Susan Treadgold
Success University for women

"Always be on the lookout, your ship may be coming in."
Anon.

"No one person changes the world. We together change the world."
Jody Williams
Chair, Nobel Women's Initiative

"Our lives are so short. And our time on this planet is so precious. All we have is each other."
Jacqueline Novogratz

"I can do anything good better than anyone. Yeah, Yeah Yeah. "
Jessica, 4 years old.

"Someday is here and now. Make the most of it."

"Someone loveable looks up to you."

"If we stop defining each other by what we are not, and start defining ourselves by who we are, we can all be a lot freer."
Emma Watson UNWomen Goodwill Ambassador

"Education is the best antidote to fear."

"Don't even think about telling me to give up."

"I am stronger than violence, oppression and fear. What are you stronger than?"

"I don't want to get to the end of my life and find that I just lived the length of it. I want to have lived the width of it as well."
Diane Ackerman

"The best thing to hold onto in life is each other."
Audrey Hepburn

"I will never give in to old age until I become old. And I'm not old yet!"
Tina Turner

"I believe in you more than you believe in yourself. But one day that will change. And you will inspire someone else to believe in themselves. This is the cycle."

"Rules? What rules?"

"Don't just stand there. Be someone."

"A beautiful face will age and a perfect body will change, but a beautiful soul will always be a beautiful soul.
Believe in yourself and your dreams."
Jean Ann Reuter

"The only way we get change is when enough people in this country say I'm mad as hell and I'm fed up and I'm not going to do this anymore."

Elizabeth Warren

"You can imprison a man, but not an idea.
You can exile a man, but not an idea.
You can kill a man, but not an idea."
Benazir Bhutto

"Sometimes all it takes is someone to believe in you for you to believe in yourself."
Sandra Galati

"If you could see in yourself what I see in you, the transformation in your results would amaze and humble you."

"As a man changes his own nature, so does the attitude of the world change towards him. This is the divine mystery surpreme. We need not wait to see what others do."
Mahatma Gandhi

"The cure for boredom is curiosity.
There is no cure for curiosity."
Dorothy Parker

"Have faith. Whatever you choose will be the best and the right choice."
Molly Cantrell-Kraig

"We always choose the path of least resistance. It just looks difficult to others sometimes."

"I want for myself what I want for other women. Absolute equality."
Agnes Macphail

"I'm not a one-in-a-million kind of girl.
I'm a once-in-a-lifetime kind of woman."
Anon.

"Nothing lasts forever. That is why everything is so precious."
Susan Macaulay

"I'm not bossy, I just have better ideas."

"When you see something wrong, do something."

"Success is your ability to regain your composure quickly after losing it."

"How we respond to the world shows our character and our resilience."

"I want to do it because I want to do it."
Amelia Earhart

"Your self emerges more clearly over time."
Meryl Streep

"Can anything be sadder than work left unfinished? Yes. Work never begun."
Christina Rossetti

"The price of being yourself, is dealing with other people's angst about it."
Whoopi Goldberg

"I was raised to be an independent woman, not the victim of anything."
Kamala Harris

"If a woman wants be a legend, she should just go ahead and be one."
Calamity Jane

"There is no age limit for life pleasures."
Annette Bridges

"Remake yourself into something better with the broken pieces of your life." **@Kopcarrillo**

"Think about what made you happy as a child and rediscover it. It's who you were meant to be."
@carolynfrith

"Keep it simple. Keep it positive. Keep it real."
@uhyeahlicious

"Watch your negative thoughts and stay true to your vision and purpose."
@Womenworking

"People often judge me on my past, but hardly ever ask what I've learnt from it."
Unknown

"Self reliance is a masterful teacher. The greatest lessons come from one's own mistakes."
@DrRobyn

"It's nice to be important. But it's much more important to be nice."
@thesubtlemaura

"You can judge big people by how they judge little people.
@AineBelton

"I like people who speak their minds, u never have to play guessing games w them."
@Kopcarrillo

"Want to save the world? Start with a smile!"
@Her_Lioness